EVERYMAN,
I WILL GO WITH THEE
AND BE THY GUIDE,
IN THY MOST NEED
TO GO BY THY SIDE

RUMI
POEMS

· · · · · · · · · · · · · · · · · ·

SELECTED AND EDITED BY
PETER WASHINGTON

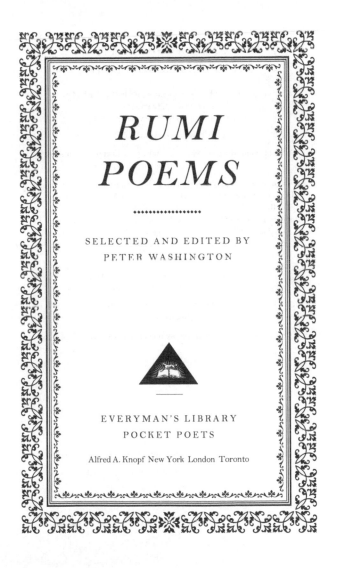

EVERYMAN'S LIBRARY
POCKET POETS

Alfred A. Knopf New York London Toronto

THIS IS A BORZOI BOOK

PUBLISHED BY ALFRED A. KNOPF

This selection by Peter Washington first published in
Everyman's Library, 2006
Copyright © 2006 by Everyman's Library

Nineteenth printing (US)

A list of acknowledgments to copyright owners appears at the back
of this volume.

All rights reserved. Published in the United States by Alfred A. Knopf,
a division of Penguin Random House LLC, New York, and in Canada by
Penguin Random House Canada Limited, Toronto. Distributed by Penguin
Random House LLC, New York. Published in the United Kingdom by
Everyman's Library, 50 Albemarle Street, London W1S 4BD and
distributed by Penguin Random House UK,
20 Vauxhall Bridge Road, London SW1V 2SA.

www.randomhouse.com/everymans
www.everymanslibrary.co.uk

ISBN 978-0-307-26352-0 (US)
978-1-84159-769-0 (UK)

A CIP catalogue record for this book is available from the British Library

Typography by Peter B. Willberg

Typeset in the UK by AccComputing, North Barrow, Somerset

Printed and bound in Germany by GGP Media GmbH, Pössneck

CONTENTS

Foreword   11

The guest house   17
And he is with us   18
Come, beggars   19
My worst habit   20
The marriage of true minds..   21
You and I   22
The friend who said 'I'   23
The phrasing must change   25
Saladin's begging bowl   27
One by one   29
A community of the spirit   32
Look at love   34
How long will you hide   36
Quatrains..   38
Of being woven   41
Clothes abandoned on the shore   43
The diver's clothes lying empty   45
The root of the root of your Self   46
Does personality survive?   48
All my friends   51
The fragrant air   52
Don't be bitter my friend   53
The waterwheel   54

Search the darkness 55
In every breath 56
A mouse and a frog 58
Quatrains 60
The weeping flute 63
What a man can say 64
The world which is made of our love for
emptiness 65
I am the slave who set the master free 66
Restless 67
Quietness 69
The perfect man 70
The true Ṣūfi 72
The birds of Solomon 73
Love and fear 74
If you don't have 76
The pull of love 78
Elegy for Sana'i 80
Quatrains 81
Story water 85
The soul of prayer 87
The bird on the city-wall 88
'Here am I' 89
Solomon's crooked crown 90
The evil in ourselves 91
The blind follower 93
The Sufi in the orchard 94

The truth within us 95
The treasure-seeker 96
Gnats inside the wind 98
The far mosque 99
The monk who searched for a man 100
The thief in the orchard 101
Fine feathers 102
The foal that would not drink 103
An empty garlic 104
The camel, the ox and the ram 105
The man who stole a snake, on the answer
     to prayer 106
Galen and the madman 107
Omar and the man who thought he saw
     the new moon 108
Red shirt 109
The grammarian and the boatman 110
The three brothers and the Chinese princess .. 111
Quatrains 119
If you stay awake 122
Asleep to the world 124
Reality and appearance 126
God in nature 127
Amor agitat molem 129
Immediate knowledge 130
Mystics know 132
The relativity of evil 134

The soul of goodness in things evil 136
Good words 137
The complete artist 138
An awkward comparison 139
Spiritual churning 140
The necessary foil 141
Tradition and intuition 142
Someone digging in the ground 143
The elephant in the dark, on the reconciliation
    of contrarieties 144
The ladder to heaven 145
Love is reckless 147
Feeling and thinking 148
Tending two shops 149
The parable of the anxious cow 151
The greedy wife and the cat 152
The dog in the doorway 153
The carnal soul 155
Acts of helplessness 156
Mystical perception 158
The world of time 160
Quatrains 161
The mouse and the camel 164
My secret beloved 166
This is love 168
Only you 169
You are my life 171

Talking through the door 172
As your sword 175
Sweep the dust off the sea 176
You ask me 178
The wine of love 180
You are drunk 181
A great wagon 184
You are 185
Did I not say to you 187
Quatrains 189
The divine factory 193
Chickpea to cook 194
The uses of tribulation 196
You have seized me by the ear 199
Enough words? 200
Die now 202
Remembered music 203
Do you break our harp, exalted one 205
The flute weeps 206
Everywhere 208
I am 210
Whatever happens 213
If a tree could move on foot or wing 215
Where everything is music 217
The unseen power 219
Song of the reed 220
If you can only reflect 223

The ascending soul 224
The progress of Man 225
Where did it all go 227
The negative way 228
Dissolver of sugar 230
The heart is like a grain of corn 231
Quatrains 232
Deification 235
We came whirling 237
Two discourses 239

Acknowledgments 251

FOREWORD

Jalal al-Din, known as *Rumi* (i.e., from Rum) or *Mawlana* (Master), was born in 1207 at Balkh in northern Afghanistan. In 1228 he moved with his family to Konya, seat of the Seljuk empire and a centre of learning more than equal to anything in the West at that time. Two years later he succeeded his father as teacher and preacher there. Some idea of his pedagogic style can be found in the discourses at the end of this volume.

Introduced to Islamic mysticism by an old student of his father's, in 1244 he encountered the wandering dervish Shams al-Din of Tabriz to whom he became devoted. Shams, who inspired much of Rumi's poetry, disappeared in 1247, possibly murdered by the poet's jealous pupils. Although Rumi formed other close relationships, his love for Shams remained the central experience of his life, as described in the *Divani-i Shams-i Tabriz*, in which many of his most celebrated poems appear.

Under the influence of mystical traditions already several centuries old, Rumi founded the Mevlevi Order (the dancing dervishes) and expounded Sufism in the lyrical outpourings of the *Divan*, the epigrams of the *Ruba'iyat* (Quatrains), and the more dogmatic verses of the *Mathnawi-i Ma'nawi*, a vast collection of fables and meditations in 27,000 couplets. Letters also survive.

11

He died in 1273 and his burial place in Konya remains a shrine to this day.

For Rumi, poetry, philosophy and theology are united in the theosophy – divine wisdom – of Sufism. Some commentators (including at least one of the translators represented in this book) have suggested that Sufism is beyond analysis or direct exposition. On this view, it can be communicated only indirectly, if at all, through dance, music, fable and metaphor. More mundane scholars have attempted explications. Among these, the preface to *Rumi, Poet and Mystic* by Reynold A. Nicholson remains the best brief English introduction to the poet's work after more than half a century.

Describing Rumi as a pantheist, a monist and a mystic, Nicholson identifies the following propositions in his writing: that all being is in essence One; that this essence is manifested continuously, not in a single act of creation; that God is absolute, immanent and transcendent; that His essence is unknowable except obliquely through the names and attributes of the phenomenal world; that the purpose of creation is for God to know Himself; and that the Sufi or Perfect Man – as exemplified in Mohammed and the line of prophets to which he belongs – comes nearest to the realization of divine self-knowledge in human life. All these propositions will be found in the following poems.

However, Nicholson is careful to point out that Rumi's theosophy is not organized in any strictly logical or developmental way. He is a teacher, concerned with the practice of religion more than the theory. Furthermore, his poems are not aesthetic ends in themselves but signs of an ineffable reality. In spite of this, some recent epigones have felt free to select what they like from Rumi's work, deploying it for therapeutic, devotional or even erotic purposes of their own.

Nicholson and Arberry, the British scholars on whose versions of the text many later anglophone translators still rely, took an altogether more respectful approach. For them, the meaning of the text was paramount, even at the expense of verbal felicity. In this selection we present different modes of translation, ranging from the near-literal to what Dryden called imitation – the free rendering of an old text in new terms. If Nicholson and Arberry represent one extreme, Coleman Barks and Andrew Harvey can be found at the other, the rest somewhere in between. Occasionally I have offered the same poem in different versions. Readers will decide which they prefer.

Persian speakers seem to be agreed that the complex and subtle music of Rumi's verse is beyond adequate translation. Even his dogmas – if that is the right word – can be hard to render succinctly. Although Everyman Pocket Poets usually dispense with academic apparatus,

I have made an exception in this case, including samples of notes attached to the Nicholson translations, in order to give readers ignorant of Islam some guidance to the unfamiliar context of Rumi's verse and an idea of the complexity and subtlety underlying poems which may appear simple on the surface. That said, any reader familiar with Donne or Hopkins will recognize the combination of spiritual intensity, erotic imagery, intellectual reach, personal commitment and technical virtuosity which characterizes these poems.

Initials at the end of each poem indicate the translator. Sources are provided at the end of the book. We have preserved the different styles of punctuation, spelling and grammar found in each translation. Persian poems do not have individual titles. These have been supplied by translators or, in one or two cases, by the editor.

Peter Washington

RUMI

Anywhere you find a lullaby
Leave; safety's final danger.
When you come across a story-teller –
Know a house is being destroyed.

AH

Live in the nowhere that you came from,
even though you have an address here.

CB

This flute is played with fire, not with wind...

KH

THE GUEST HOUSE

This being human is a guest house.
Every morning a new arrival.

A joy, a depression, a meanness,
some momentary awareness comes
as an unexpected visitor.

Welcome and entertain them all!
Even if they're a crowd of sorrows,
who violently sweep your house
empty of its furniture,
still, treat each guest honorably.
He may be clearing you out
for some new delight.

The dark thought, the shame, the malice,
meet them at the door laughing,
and invite them in.

Be grateful for whoever comes,
because each has been sent
as a guide from beyond.

CB

AND HE IS WITH US

Totally unexpected my guest arrived.
'Who is it?' asked my heart.
'The face of the moon,' said my soul.

As he entered the house,
we all ran into the street madly looking for the moon.
'I'm in here,' he was calling from inside,
but we were calling him outside unaware of his call.
Our drunken nightingale is singing in the garden,
and we are cooing like doves, 'Where, where, where?'

A crowd formed: 'Where's the thief?'
And the thief among us is saying,
'Yeah, where's the thief.'
All our voices became mixed together
and not one voice stood out from the others.

And He is with you means He is searching with you.
He is nearer to you than yourself. Why look outside?
Become like melting snow; wash yourself of yourself.
With love your inner voice will find a tongue
growing like a silent white lily in the heart.

KH

COME, BEGGARS

come, beggars
sit with open hands
at the gate
of nothingness

God will bring bread
without the medium
of bread

sweetness
without honey or bee

when past and future
dissolve
there is only you

senseless as a lute
upon the breast of God

DL

MY WORST HABIT

My worst habit is I get so tired of winter
I become a torture to those I'm with.

If you're not here, nothing grows.
I lack clarity. My words
tangle and knot up.

How to cure bad water? Send it back to the river.
How to cure bad habits? Send me back to you.

When water gets caught in habitual whirlpools,
dig a way out through the bottom
to the ocean. There is a secret medicine
given only to those who hurt so hard
they can't hope.

The hopers would feel slighted if they knew.

Look as long as you can at the friend you love,
no matter whether that friend is moving away from you
or coming back toward you.

CB

THE MARRIAGE OF TRUE MINDS

Happy the moment when we are seated in the palace,
    thou and I,
With two forms and with two figures but with one
    soul, thou and I.
The colours of the grove and the voices of the birds
    will bestow immortality
At the time when we shall come into the garden,
    thou and I.
The stars of Heaven will come to gaze upon us:
We shall show them the moon herself, thou and I.
Thou and I, individuals no more, shall be mingled
    in ecstasy,
Joyful and secure from foolish babble, thou and I.
All the bright-plumed birds of Heaven will devour
    their hearts with envy
In the place where we shall laugh in such a fashion,
    thou and I.
This is the greatest wonder, that thou and I,
    sitting here in the same nook,
Are at this moment both in 'Irāq and Khorāsān,
    thou and I.

RAN

YOU AND I

A moment of happiness,
you and I sitting on the verandah,
apparently two, but one in soul, you and I.

We feel the flowing water of life here,
you and I, with the garden's beauty and the birds
        singing.
The stars will be watching us,
and we will show them
what it means to be a thin crescent moon.

You and I unselfed, will be together,
indifferent to idle speculation, you and I.
The parrots of heaven will be cracking sugar
as we laugh together, you and I.

And what is even more amazing
is that while here together, you and I
are at this very moment in Iraq and Khorasan.
In one form upon this earth,
and in another form in a timeless sweet land.

KH

THE FRIEND WHO SAID 'I'[1]

A certain man knocked at his friend's door: his friend
    asked, 'Who is there?'
He answered, 'I.' 'Begone,' said his friend, ''tis too
    soon: at my table there is no place for the raw.'
How shall the raw one be cooked but in the fire of
    absence? What else will deliver him from
    hypocrisy?
He turned sadly away, and for a whole year the flames
    of separation consumed him;
Then he came back and again paced to and fro beside
    the house of his friend.
He knocked at the door with a hundred fears and
    reverences, lest any disrespectful word might
    escape from his lips.
'Who is there?' cried his friend. He answered, 'Thou,
    O charmer of all hearts!'
'Now,' said the friend, 'since thou art I, come in: there
    is no room for two I's in this house.
The double end of thread is not for the needle:
    inasmuch as thou art single, enter the needle.'[2]

---

1 *Math.* I, 3056. Mystical union involves a transformation of the
lover's personality into that of the Beloved.
2 The mystic becomes 'single' when he ceases to be conscious of
himself as an *alter ego* beside God, who is the only real Ego.

'Tis the thread that enters the needle: the needle's eye
    will not admit the camel.[3]
How shall the camel be fined down save by the shears
    of asceticism?[4]

RAN

---

3 Unbelievers 'will not enter Paradise till the camel passes through
the needle's eye' (*Qur'ān* VII, 38). Cf. St Matthew XIX, 24.
4 The carnal nature is symbolized by a thorn-eating camel.

THE PHRASING MUST CHANGE

Learn about your inner self from those who know such
    things,
but don't repeat verbatim what they say.
Zuleikha let everything be the name of Joseph, from
    celery seed
to aloes wood. She loved him so much she concealed
    his name
in many different phrases, the inner meanings
known only to her. When she said, *The wax is softening
near the fire*, she meant, My love is wanting me.
Or if she said, *Look, the moon is up* or *The willow has
    new leaves*
or *The branches are trembling* or *The coriander seeds
have caught fire* or *The roses are opening*
or *The king is in a good mood today* or *Isn't that lucky?*
or *The furniture needs dusting* or
The water carrier is here or *It's almost daylight* or
These vegetables are perfect or *The bread needs more salt*
or *The clouds seem to be moving against the wind*
or *My head hurts* or *My headache's better*,
anything she praises, it's Joseph's touch she means,
any complaint, it's his being away.
When she's hungry, it's for him. Thirsty, his name is
    a sherbet.
Cold, he's a fur. This is what the Friend can do

when one is in such love. Sensual people use
        the holy names
often, but they don't work for them.
The miracle Jesus did by being the name of God,
Zuleikha felt in the name of *Joseph*.

When one is united to the core of another, to speak
        of that
is to breathe the name *Hu*, empty of self and filled
with love. As the saying goes, *The pot drips what is in it.*
The saffron spice of connecting, laughter.
The onion smell of separation, crying.
Others have many things and people they love.
This is not the way of Friend and friend.

CB

SALADIN'S BEGGING BOWL

Of these two thousand 'I' and 'We' people,
which am I?

Don't try to keep me from asking!
Listen, when I'm this out of control!
But don't put anything breakable in my way!

There is an original inside me.
What's here is a mirror for that, for you.

If you are joyful, I am.
If you grieve, or if you're bitter, or graceful,
I take on those qualities.

Like the shadow of a cypress tree in the meadow,
like the shadow of a rose, I live
close to the rose.

If I separated myself from you,
I would turn entirely thorn.

Every second, I drink another cup of my own
    blood-wine.
Every instant, I break an empty cup against your door.

I reach out, wanting you to tear me open.

Saladin's generosity lights a candle in my chest.
Who *am* I then?
His empty begging bowl.

CB

ONE BY ONE

one by one
our friends
filled with joy and quest
begin to arrive

one by one our friends
the worshipers of ecstasy
begin to arrive

more friends and sweethearts
filling you with love
are on their way

darlings of spring
journeying from gardens
begin to arrive

one by one
living their destiny
in this world

the ones who are gone are gone
but the ones who survived
begin to arrive

all their pockets
filled with gold
from endless treasures

bringing gifts
for the needy of the world
begin to arrive

the weak and the exhausted
the frightened by love
will be gone

the rejuvenated
the healthy and happy
begin to arrive

the pure souls
like the spectrums
of the shining sun

descending from the high heavens
to lowly earth
begin to arrive

luscious and happy
the blessed garden
whose heavenly fruits

spring forth
from the virgin winter
begin to arrive

those who are born
from the roots
of generosity and love

taking a journey
from paradise to paradise
begin to arrive

NK

A COMMUNITY OF THE SPIRIT

There is a community of the spirit.
Join it, and feel the delight
of walking in the noisy street,
and *being* the noise.

Drink *all* your passion,
and be a disgrace.

Close both eyes
to see with the other eye.

Open your hands,
if you want to be held.

Sit down in this circle.

Quit acting like a wolf, and feel
the shepherd's love filling you.

At night, your beloved wanders.
Don't accept consolations.

Close your mouth against food.
Taste the lover's mouth in yours.

You moan, 'She left me.' 'He left me.'
Twenty more will come.

Be empty of worrying.
Think of who created thought!

Why do you stay in prison
when the door is so wide open?

Move outside the tangle of fear-thinking.
Live in silence.

Flow down and down in always
widening rings of being.

CB

LOOK AT LOVE

look at love
how it tangles
with the one fallen in love

look at spirit
how it fuses with earth
giving it new life

why are you so busy
with this or that or good or bad
pay attention to how things blend

why talk about all
the known and the unknown
see how unknown merges into the known

why think separately
of this life and the next
when one is born from the last

look at your heart and tongue
one feels but deaf and dumb
the other speaks in words and signs

look at water and fire
earth and wind
enemies and friends all at once

the wolf and the lamb
the lion and the deer
far away yet together

look at the unity of this
spring and winter
manifested in the equinox

you too must mingle my friends
since the earth and the sky
are mingled just for you and me

be like sugarcane
sweet yet silent
don't get mixed up with bitter words

my beloved grows
right out of my own heart
how much more union can there be

NK

HOW LONG WILL YOU HIDE

how long will you hide
your beautiful
festive smile

teach your laughter
to a flower
manifest an eternity

why do you think
the door to the sky
is closed on your face

it allures and invites
your magical touch
to open and arrive

an entire caravan
is waiting in ecstasy
for your coming and leading

come on my friend
use your talisman and
harness all their souls

today is the day to unite
with your longing beloved
wait no more
for an unknown tomorrow

a tambourine is in a corner
begging your playing hands
a flute is sitting dormant
begging your happy lips

NK

QUATRAINS

Pale sunlight,
pale the wall.

Love moves away.
The light changes.

I need more grace
than I thought.

***

I would love to kiss you.
The price of kissing is your life.

Now my loving is running toward my life shouting,
What a bargain, let's buy it.

***

You have said what you are.
I am what I am.
Your actions in my head,
my head here in my hands
with something circling inside.
I have no name
for what circles
so perfectly.

***

Daylight, full of small dancing particles
and the one great turning, our souls
are dancing with you, without feet, they dance.
Can you see them when I whisper in your ear?

***

They try to say what you are, spiritual or sexual?
They wonder about Solomon and all his wives.

In the body of the world, they say, there is a soul
and you are that.

But we have ways within each other
that will never be said by anyone.

***

Come to the orchard in Spring.
There is light and wine, and sweethearts
        in the pomegranate flowers.

If you do not come, these do not matter.
If you do come, these do not matter.

***

Walk to the well.
Turn as the earth and the moon turn,
circling what they love.
Whatever circles comes from the center.

***

I circle your nest tonight,
around and around until morning
when a breath of air says, *Now,*
and the Friend holds up like a goblet
some anonymous skull.

***

No better love than love with no object,
no more satisfying work than work with no purpose.

If you could give up tricks and cleverness,
that would be the cleverest trick!

CB

OF BEING WOVEN

'The way is full of genuine sacrifice.

The thickets blocking the path are anything
that keeps you from that, any fear
that you may be broken to bits like a glass bottle.
This road demands courage and stamina,

yet it's full of footprints! Who *are*
these companions? They are rungs
in your ladder. Use them!
With company you quicken your ascent.

You may be happy enough going along,
but with others you'll get farther, and faster.

Someone who goes cheerfully by himself
to the customs house to pay his traveler's tax
will go even more lightheartedly
when friends are with him.

Every prophet sought out companions.
A wall standing alone is useless,
but put three or four walls together,
and they'll support a roof and keep
the grain dry and safe.

When ink joins with a pen, then the blank paper
can say something. Rushes and reeds must be *woven*
to be useful as a mat. If they weren't interlaced,
the wind would blow them away.

Like that, God paired up
creatures, and gave them friendship.'

This is how the fowler and the bird were arguing
about hermitic living and Islam.

It's a prolonged debate.
Husam, shorten their controversy.
Make the *Mathnawi* more nimble and less lumbering.
Agile sounds are more appealing to the heart's ear.

CB

CLOTHES ABANDONED ON THE SHORE

Your body is here with us,
but your heart is in the meadow.
You travel with the hunters
though you yourself are what they hunt.

Like a reed flute,
you are encased by your body,
with a restless breathy sound inside.

You are a diver;
your body is just clothing left at the shore.
You are a fish whose way is through water.

In this sea there are many bright veins
and some that are dark.
The heart receives its light
from those bright veins.

If you lift your wing
I can show them to you.
You are hidden like the blood within,
and you are shy to the touch.

Those same veins sing a melancholy tune
in the sweet-stringed lute,
music from a shoreless sea
whose waves roar out of infinity.

KH

THE DIVER'S CLOTHES LYING EMPTY

You're sitting here with us, but you're also out walking
in a field at dawn. You are yourself
the animal we hunt when you come with us on the hunt.
You're in your body like a plant is solid in the ground,
yet you're wind. You're the diver's clothes
lying empty on the beach. You're the fish.

In the ocean are many bright strands
and many dark strands like veins that are seen
when a wing is lifted up.
Your hidden self is blood in those, those veins
that are lute strings that make ocean music,
not the sad edge of surf, but the sound of no shore.

CB

THE ROOT OF THE ROOT OF YOUR SELF

Don't go away, come near.
Don't be faithless, be faithful.
Find the antidote in the venom.
Come to the root of the root of your Self.

Molded of clay, yet kneaded
from the substance of certainty,
a guard at the Treasury of Holy Light –
come, return to the root of the root of your Self.

Once you get hold of selflessness,
you'll be dragged from your ego
and freed from many traps.
Come, return to the root of the root of your Self.

You are born from the children of God's creation,
but you have fixed your sight too low.
How can you be happy?
Come, return to the root of the root of your Self.

Although you are a talisman protecting a treasure,
you are also the mine.
Open your hidden eyes
and come to the root of the root of your Self.

You were born from a ray of God's majesty
and have the blessings of a good star.
Why suffer at the hands of things that don't exist?
Come, return to the root of the root of your Self.

You are a ruby embedded in granite.
How long will you pretend it isn't true?
We can see it in your eyes.
Come to the root of the root of your Self.

You came here from the presence of that fine Friend,
a little drunk, but gentle, stealing our hearts
with that look so full of fire; so,
come, return to the root of the root of your Self.

Our master and host, Shamsi Tabrizi,
has put the eternal cup before you.
Glory be to God, what a rare wine!
So come, return to the root of the root of your Self.

KH

DOES PERSONALITY SURVIVE?[1]

There is no dervish in the world; and if there be, that
   dervish is really non-existent.[2]
He exists in respect of the survival of his essence, but
   his attributes are extinguished in the Attributes
   of God.[3]
Like the flame of a candle in the presence of the sun,
   he is really non-existent, though he exists in
   formal calculation.

---

1 *Math.* III, 3669. The term *fanā* is used by Ṣūfīs in connexion with
different theories as to the nature of mystical union and may imply:
(1) that the *essence* of the creature (*dhāt-i ʿabd*) passes away (*fānī
   shavad*) in the Essence of God and ceases to exist, just as a drop
   of water loses its individuality (*taʿayyun*) in the ocean;
(2) that the *attributes* of the creature (*ṣifāt-i ʿabd*) pass away in the
   Attributes of God: his human attributes are changed (*mubaddal*)
   into Divine Attributes so that God becomes his ear and eye;
(3) that the *essence* of the creature vanishes in the Light of the Divine
   Essence, like the disappearance of stars in the light of the sun.
   His creatureliness (*khalqiyyah*) does not cease to exist, but is
   concealed (*makhfī*) under the aspect of Creativeness (*Ḥaqqiyyah*):
   the Lord (*Rabb*) is manifest, the slave (*ʿabd*) invisible.
2 Here 'dervish' stands for the perfect type of spiritual poverty, the
saint who is denuded of self and dead to the world, even if he appears
to live in it.
3 Nominally he exists, for his 'person' (*dhāt-i bashariyyah*) is not
annihilated; but since it has been transfigured and 'deified', he is really
non-existent as an individual and only survives (*bāqī hast*) in virtue
of the Divine Life and Energy which constitute his whole being.

The flame's essence is existent in so far as if you put
    cotton upon it, the cotton will be consumed;
But in reality it is non-existent: it gives you no light,
    the sun has naughted it.
When an ounce of vinegar is dissolved in a hundred
    maunds of sugar
The acid flavour is non-existent when you taste the
    sugar, albeit the ounce exists as a surplus when
    you weigh.
In the presence of a lion the deer becomes senseless:
    her existence is but a veil for his.
Analogies drawn by imperfect men concerning the
    action of the Lord are like the emotion of love,
    they are not irreverent.
The lover's pulse bounds up unabashed, he levels
    himself with the King.
He appears irreverent, for his claim of love involves
    equality with the Beloved;
But look deeper: what does he claim? Both he and his
    claim are naughted in the presence of that Sultan.
Māta Zayd^{un} (Zayd died): if Zayd is the agent
    (grammatical subject), yet he is not the agent,
    since he is defunct.

49

He is the agent only in respect of the grammatical
    expression; otherwise he is the one acted upon,
    and Death is his slayer.
What ability to act remains in one who has been so
    overpowered that all the qualities of an agent are
    gone from him?

RAN

ALL MY FRIENDS

all my friends
departed like dreams
left alone
i called upon
one friend
to become
my entire dream

this is the one
who soothes my heart
with endless
tenderness and love

the one who
one hour bestows
inner peace
and the next
the nectar of life

this dream too
as it arrives
i come alive and
as it departs
i'm helpless again

NK

THE FRAGRANT AIR

the fragrant air
steals the water
from the cistern

each breath pilfers
a fragment of soul
to another world

suddenly
this body is still
like sea-scum
come to rest on the shore

death is shouting
and beating his drum

death is hoarse from shouting

the drum of death
is split
by amazing blows

as you slip beneath the waves
like a shipload of dung

DL

DON'T BE BITTER MY FRIEND

don't be bitter my friend
you'll regret it soon
hold to your togetherness
or surely you'll scatter

don't walk away gloomy
from this garden
you'll end up like an owl
dwelling in old ruins

face the war and
be a warrior like a lion
or you'll end up like a pet
tucked away in a stable

once you conquer
your selfish self
all your darkness
will change to light

NK

THE WATERWHEEL

Stay together, friends.
Don't scatter and sleep.

Our friendship is made
of being awake.

The waterwheel accepts water
and turns and gives it away,
weeping.

That way it stays in the garden,
whereas another roundness rolls
through a dry riverbed looking
for what it thinks it wants.

Stay here, quivering with each moment
like a drop of mercury.

CB

SEARCH THE DARKNESS

Sit with your friends; don't go back to sleep.
Don't sink like a fish to the bottom of the sea.

Surge like an ocean,
don't scatter yourself like a storm.

Life's waters flow from darkness.
Search the darkness, don't run from it.

Night travelers are full of light,
and you are, too; don't leave this companionship.

Be a wakeful candle in a golden dish,
don't slip into the dirt like quicksilver.

The moon appears for night travelers,
be watchful when the moon is full.

KH

IN EVERY BREATH

in every breath
if you're the center
of your own desires
you'll lose the grace
of your beloved

but if in every breath
you blow away
your self claim
the ecstasy of love
will soon arrive

in every breath
if you're the center
of your own thoughts
the sadness of autumn
will fall on you

but if in every breath
you strip naked
just like a winter
the joy of spring
will grow from within

all your impatience
comes from the push
for gain of patience
let go of the effort
and peace will arrive

all your unfulfilled desires
are from your greed
for gain of fulfillments
let go of them all
and they will be sent as gifts

fall in love with
the agony of love
not the ecstasy
then the beloved
will fall in love with you

NK

A MOUSE AND A FROG

A mouse and a frog meet every morning on
    the riverbank.
They sit in a nook of the ground and talk.

Each morning, the second they see each other,
they open easily, telling stories and dreams
    and secrets,
empty of any fear or suspicious holding back.

To watch and listen to those two
is to understand how, as it's written,
sometimes when two beings come together,
Christ becomes visible.

The mouse starts laughing out a story he hasn't
    thought of
in five years, and the telling might take five years!
There's no blocking the speechflow-river-running-
all-carrying momentum that true intimacy is.

Bitterness doesn't have a chance
with those two.

The God-messenger, Khidr, touches a roasted fish.
It leaps off the grill back into the water.

Friend sits by Friend, and the tablets appear.
They read the mysteries
off each other's foreheads.

But one day the mouse complains, 'There are times
when I want *sohbet*, and you're out in the water,
jumping around where you can't hear me.

We meet at this appointed time,
but the text says, *Lovers pray constantly.*

Once a day, once a week, five times an hour,
is not enough. Fish like we are
need the ocean around us!'

Do camel bells say, *Let's meet back here Thursday night*?
Ridiculous. They jingle
together continuously,
talking while the camel walks.

Do you pay regular visits to *yourself*?
Don't argue or answer rationally.

Let us die,
                and dying, reply.

CB

QUATRAINS

Never think the earth void or dead –
It's a hare, awake with shut eyes:
It's a sauce-pan, simmering with broth –
One clear look, you'll see it's in ferment.

***

What do you hope to find
In the soul's streets
In the bloody streets of the heart
That have no news, even of yourself?

***

Ignorant men are the soul's enemy
Shatter the jar of smug words
Cling for life to those who know
Prop a mirror in water, it rusts

***

How long will we fill our pockets
Like children with dirt and stones?
Let the world go. Holding it
We never know ourselves, never are air-born.

***

I lost my world, my fame, my mind –
The Sun appeared, and all the shadows ran.
I ran after them, but vanished as I ran –
Light ran after me and hunted me down.

***

Circle the Sun, you become a sun:
Circle a Master, and you become one.
You'd be a ruby, if you danced round this mine –
Dance round him, you'll glitter like gold.

***

Atom, you want to flee the sun?
Madman, give up!
You're a jar; fate's a stone –
Kick against it, you'll waste your wine.

***

I was once, like you, 'enlightened', 'rational',
I too scoffed at lovers.
Now I am drunk, crazed, thin with misery –
No-one's safe! Watch out!

***

Reason, leave now! You'll not find wisdom here!
Were you thin as a hair, there'd still be no room.
The Sun is risen! In its vast dazzle
Every lamp is drowned.

***

Body of earth, don't talk of earth
Tell the story of pure mirrors
The Creator has given you this splendour –
Why talk of anything else?

***

This body's a mirror of heaven:
Its energies make angels jealous.
Our purity astounds seraphim:
Devils shiver at our nerve.

***

Suddenly, he is here –
Heads touch, secrets start singing.
Time's barn is flattened by storm-wind
We crumple on its straw like drunks.

AH

THE WEEPING FLUTE

the weeping flute
remembers
the riverbed

the stick beats the drum,
    'I was once green,
        a living branch.'

the skin on the lute
trembles
like living flesh

the lovers turn
bewildered
like Jacob seeking Joseph

if you heard their cries
your heart would shatter
like glass

DL

WHAT A MAN CAN SAY

In the name of friendship,
don't repeat to my Beloved
all that I said last night,
out of my mind;
but if, by God, she hears it,
she'll understand what a man can say
in the dark, loud or quiet, rough or soft,
when reason is not at home.
If God let this anxiety out,
no one in the world will stay sane.
Mind, are these your dark suggestions?
Cloud, is this your sad rain?
Believers, watch your hearts.
Curious or kind, stay away.

KH

THIS WORLD WHICH IS MADE OF
OUR LOVE FOR EMPTINESS

Praise to the emptiness that blanks out existence.
    Existence:
this place made from our love for that emptiness!
Yet somehow comes emptiness,
this existence goes.
Praise to that happening, over and over!

For years I pulled my own existence out of emptiness.
Then one swoop, one swing of the arm,
that work is over.
Free of who I was, free of presence, free of
dangerous fear, hope,
free of mountainous wanting.

CB

I AM THE SLAVE WHO SET THE
MASTER FREE

I am the slave who set the master free, I am the one
    who taught the teacher.
I am that soul which was born of the world yesterday,
    and yet erected the ancient world.
I am the wax whose claim is this, that it was I who
    made steel steel.
I have painted with surmeh many a sightless one,
    I have taught many a one without intelligence.
I am the black cloud in the night of grief who
    gladdened the day of festival.
I am the amazing earth who out of the fire of love
    filled with air the brain of the sky.
In joy that king slept not last night, because I the
    slave remembered him.
It is not to blame, since you intoxicated me, if I am
    scandalous and wrought injustice.
Silence, for the mirror is rusting over; when I blew
    upon it, it protested against me.

AJA

RESTLESS

restless
now i go to the door
now i go on the roof
till i see your face
i'll never know rest

neighbors speak of me
when you are away
as meek or mad
but when you return
everything subsides

this heart of mine
tears itself apart
and seeks no joy
but only wants to know
when you'll arrive

but when you return
and a wine-server is around
i hold a cup
fondle your hair and
caress your face

just come and see me
letting go of my wish
letting go of my pilgrimage
keeping one wish in my heart
making love to your desires

NK

QUIETNESS

Inside this new love, die.
Your way begins on the other side.
Become the sky.
Take an axe to the prison wall.
Escape.
Walk out like someone suddenly born into color.
Do it now.
You're covered with thick cloud.
Slide out the side. Die,
and be quiet. Quietness is the surest sign
that you've died.
Your old life was a frantic running
from silence.

The speechless full moon
comes out now.

CB

THE PERFECT MAN[1]

The Quṭb is the lion: it is his business to hunt:
      all the rest eat his leavings.
So far as you can, endeavour to satisfy him, so that he
      may gain strength and hunt the wild beasts.[2]
When he is ailing, the people starve: all food comes
      from the hand of Reason.
Their spiritual experiences are only his leavings.
      Bear this in mind, if you desire the prey.
He is like Reason, they are as members of the body;
      the management of the body depends on Reason.[3]
His infirmity is of the body, not of the spirit:
      the weakness lies in the Ark, not in Noah.

1 *Math.* V, 2339. The term *Quṭb* (Pole), as used here, denotes the
Perfect Man generally and does not refer specifically to the Head
of the Ṣūfī hierarchy.
2 'Endeavour to satisfy him,' *i.e.* 'serve him faithfully, relieve his
bodily wants, and take care not to disturb him, so that he may be
left free to pursue the realities (*asrār ū ma'ānī*) which are his
spiritual food. That this is what Rūmī means by 'the wild beasts'
cannot be doubted. Giordano Bruno in his allegory of Actaeon
(*The Heroic Enthusiasts*, tr. Williams, vol. I, p. 91) not only employs
the same phrase but explains it as signifying 'the intelligible kinds
of ideal conceptions, which are occult, followed by few, visited
but rarely, and which do not disclose themselves to all those who
seek them'.
3 The Quṭb, being 'the form of Universal Reason', is the manager
(*mudabbir*) of the world. Without his mediation, it would not be
spiritually fed.

The Quṭb revolves round himself, while round him
    revolve all the spheres of Heaven.
Lend some assistance in repairing his bodily ship:
    be his chosen slave and devoted servant.
In reality your aid is a benefit to you, not to him:
    God hath said, 'If ye help God, ye will be helped.'[4]

RAN

4 *Qur'ān* LXVII, 8.

THE TRUE ṢŪFĪ[1]

What makes the Ṣūfī? Purity of heart;
Not the patched mantle and the lust perverse
Of those vile earth-bound men who steal his name.
He in all dregs discerns the essence pure:
In hardship ease, in tribulation joy.
The phantom sentries, who with batons drawn
Guard Beauty's palace-gate and curtained bower,
Give way before him, unafraid he passes,
And showing the King's arrow, enters in.[2]

RAN

1 *Math.* V, 358.
2 An arrow inscribed with the king's name was handed to a
surrendering enemy in token that his safety was guaranteed. Sa'dī
alludes to this custom in the verse:
   'Either thou wilt shoot a deadly arrow at my wounded heart
   And take my life, or thou wilt give me the arrow of indemnity
     (*tīr-i amān*).'

THE BIRDS OF SOLOMON[1]

The eloquence of courtly birds is a mere echo: where is
    the speech of the birds of Solomon?[2]
How wilt thou know their cries, when thou hast never
    seen Solomon for a single moment?
Far beyond East and West are spread the wings of the
    bird whose note thrills them that hear it:
From the Footstool of God to the earth and from the
    earth to the Divine Throne it moves in glory and
    majesty.
The bird that goes without this Solomon is a bat in
    love with darkness.
Make thyself familiar with Solomon, O miscreant bat,
    lest thou remain in darkness for ever.
Go but one ell in that direction, and like the ell thou
    wilt become the standard of measurement.[3]
Even by hopping lamely and limply in that direction
    thou wilt be freed from all lameness and limpness.

RAN

1 *Math.* II, 3758. Solomon was taught the bird language (*Qur'ān*
XXVII, 16). Here he represents the Perfect Man, *i.e.* the Ṣūfī *murshid*.
2 All artificial eloquence, such as court poets display in their
panegyrics, is meaningless in comparison with the mystic utterances
of those whom God has inspired.
3 Cf. the saying of Kharraqānī, 'I attained to God as soon as I set
foot on the first step of the ladder.' The Perfect Man is the ideal of
creation and the criterion by which the true value of everything is
to be judged.

LOVE AND FEAR[1]

The mystic ascends to the Throne in a moment; the
    ascetic needs a month for one day's journey.
Although, for the ascetic, one day is of great value,
    yet how should his one day be equal to *fifty
    thousand years*?[2]
In the life of the adept, every day is fifty thousand of
    the years of this world.[3]
Love (*maḥabbat*), and ardent love (*'ishq*) also, is an
    Attribute of God; Fear is an attribute of the slave
    to lust and appetite.[4]

---

1 *Math.* V, 2180, a passage contrasting the slow and painful progress
(*sulūk*) of the self-centred ascetic with the inward rapture (*jadhbah*)
which in a moment carries the mystic to his goal.
2 From *Qur'ān* LXX, 4: 'the angels and the Spirit (Gabriel) ascend
to Him on a Day whereof the span is fifty thousand years.' Ṣūfīs
interpret this text as a reference to the mystical resurrection and
ascension.
3 'The life of the adept' consists entirely in contemplation
(*mushāhadah*), and its 'days' (*ayyāmu 'llāh*) are the infinite, timeless
epiphanies (*tajalliyāt*) in which God reveals Himself to His true
lovers.
4 There is Qur'ānic authority for *maḥabbat*, but none for *'ishq*, the
key-word of Ṣūfī erotic symbolism. The stronger term, however,
appears in a Holy Tradition reported by Ḥasan of Basrah (*ob.* A.D.
728): 'God said, "When My servant devotes himself to praise and
recollection (*dhikr*) of Me and takes delight in it, I love him and he
loves Me (*'ashiqanī wa-'ashiqtuhu*)." '

Love hath five hundred wings, and every wing reaches
    from above the empyrean to beneath the earth.
The timorous ascetic runs on foot; the lovers of God
    fly more quickly than lightning.
May Divine Favour free thee from this wayfaring!
    None but the royal falcon hath found the way to
    the King.

RAN

IF YOU DON'T HAVE

if you don't have
enough madness in you
go and rehabilitate yourself

if you've lost a hundred times
the chess game of this life
be prepared to lose one more

if you're the wounded string
of a harp on this stage
play once more then resonate no more

if you're that exhausted bird
fighting a falcon for too long
make a comeback and be strong

you've carved a wooden horse
riding and calling it real
fooling yourself in life

though only a wooden horse
ride it again my friend
and gallop to the next post

you've never really listened
to what God has always
tried to tell you

yet you keep hoping
after your mock prayers
salvation will arrive

NK

THE PULL OF LOVE

When Hallaj found union with his Beloved,
it was right that it was on the gallows.

I snatched a cap's worth of cloth from his coat,
and it covered my reason, my head, and my feet.

I pulled a thorn from the fence of his garden,
and it has not stopped working its way into my heart.

One morning a little of his wine
turned my heart into a lion hunter.
It's right that this separation he helped me feel
lurks like a monster within my heart.

Yet heaven's wild and unbroken colt
was trained by the hand of his love.
Though reason is learned and has its honors,
it pawned its cap and robes for a cup of love.

Many hearts have sought refuge from this love,
but it drags and pulls them to its own refuge.

One cold day a bearskin was floating down the river.
I said to a man who had no clothes,
'Jump in and pull it out.'

But the bearskin was a live bear,
and the man who jumped in so eagerly

was caught in the clutches of what he went to grab.

'Let go of it,' I said, 'Fighting won't get you anywhere.'
'Let go of it? This coat won't let go of me!'
Silence. Just a hint. Who needs volumes of stories?

KH

ELEGY FOR SANA'I

I heard someone say. Master Sana'i is dead.
The death of such a master is no small thing.
He was not some straw pushed by the wind;
he was not water that froze in winter;
he was not a comb that broke in the hair;
he was not a seed swallowed by the earth.
He was a treasure of gold in this dustpit,
because he valued the whole world at a single
    barleycorn.
The earthly frame he tossed to earth.
Soul and reason he raised aloft.
How strangely the elixir blends with the dregs,
until it settles out within the flask.
A second soul which most humans never know,
I swear by God, he gave to his Beloved.
On a journey, it sometimes happens, my friend,
that a man of Merv or Rayy, a Roman or a Kurd,
travel together before each reaches home.
Should a mature one be the companion of youths?
Be silent as a compass, the King
has erased your name from the book of speech.

KH

QUATRAINS

Does sunset sometimes look like the sun's coming up?
Do you know what a faithful love is like?

You're crying. You say you've burned yourself.
But can you think of anyone who's not
hazy with smoke?

***

I want to hold you close like a lute,
so we can cry out with loving.

You would rather throw stones at a mirror?
I am your mirror, and here are the stones.

***

Late, by myself, in the boat of myself,
no light and no land anywhere,
cloudcover thick. I try to stay
just above the surface, yet I'm already under
and living within the ocean.

***

When I am with you, we stay up all night.
When you're not here, I can't go to sleep.

Praise God for these two insomnias!
And the difference between them.

***

The minute I heard my first love story
I started looking for you, not knowing
how blind that was.

Lovers don't finally meet somewhere.
They're in each other all along.

***

We are the mirror as well as the face in it.
We are tasting the taste this minute
of eternity. We are pain
and what cures pain, both. We are
the sweet cold water and the jar that pours.

***

When you feel your lips becoming infinite
and sweet, like the moon in a sky,
when you feel that spaciousness inside,
Shams of Tabriz will be there too.

***

The sun is love. The lover,
a speck circling the sun.

A Spring wind moves to dance
any branch that isn't dead.

***

Something opens our wings. Something
makes boredom and hurt disappear.
Someone fills the cup in front of us.
We taste only sacredness.

***

Held like this, to draw in milk,
no will, tasting clouds of milk,
never so content.

***

I stand up, and this one of me
turns into a hundred of me.
They say I circle around you.
Nonsense. I circle around me.

***

I have lived on the lip
of insanity, wanting to know reasons,
knocking on a door. It opens.
I've been knocking from the inside!

CB

STORY WATER

A story is like water
that you heat for your bath.

It takes messages between the fire
and your skin. It lets them meet,
and it cleans you!

Very few can sit down
in the middle of the fire itself
like a salamander or Abraham.
We need intermediaries.

A feeling of fullness comes,
but usually it takes some bread
to bring it.

Beauty surrounds us,
but usually we need to be walking
in a garden to know it.

The body itself is a screen
to shield and partially reveal
the light that's blazing
inside your presence.

Water, stories, the body,
all the things we do, are mediums
that hide and show what's hidden.

Study them,
and enjoy this being washed
with a secret we sometimes know
and then not.

CB

THE SOUL OF PRAYER[1]

Jalalu'l-dīn was asked, 'Is there any way to God nearer than the ritual prayer?' 'No,' he replied; 'but prayer does not consist in forms alone. Formal prayer has a beginning and an end, like all forms and bodies and everything that partakes of speech and sound; but the soul is unconditioned and infinite: it has neither beginning nor end. The prophets have shown the true nature of prayer.... Prayer is the drowning and unconsciousness of the soul, so that all these forms remain without. At that time there is no room even for Gabriel, who is pure spirit. One may say that the man who prays in this fashion is exempt from all religious obligations, since he is deprived of his reason. Absorption in the Divine Unity is the soul of prayer.'[2]

RAN

---

1 *Fīhi mā fīhi*, 15.
2 Ṣūfīs often describe 'the naughting of self-consciousness (*fanā 'u 'l-ṣifāt*)' which results from intense concentration of every faculty on God in the performance of the ritual prayer (*ṣalāt*). The Prophet is said to have declared that no *ṣalāt* is complete without the inward presence of God. To him every *ṣalāt* was a new Ascension (*mi'rāj*), in which he left even Gabriel behind.

THE BIRD ON THE CITY-WALL

A certain man one day asked a preacher, 'Most
illustrious orator of the pulpit, I have a question to put
to you. Answer my question in this congregation, lord
of all wisdom. A bird has perched on the city-wall:
which is better – its head or its tail?'

'If its face is turned to the city and its tail to the
country,' replied the preacher, 'know that its face is
better than its tail. But if its tail is towards the city
and its face to the country, be yourself the dust on its
tail, and leap away from its face!'

Every mineral that sets its face towards the
vegetable, life grows from the tree of its fortune.
Every vegetable that turns its face towards the
spiritual, like Khizr drinks from the Fountain of Life.

When the spirit in turn directs its face towards the
Beloved, it unloads its baggage in the life without end.

AJA

'HERE AM I'[1]

One night a certain man cried 'Allah!' till his lips grew
    sweet with praising Him.
The Devil said, 'O man of many words, where is the
    response "Here am I" (*labbayka*) to all this "Allah"?
Not a single response is coming from the Throne: how
    long will you say "Allah" with grim face?'
He was broken-hearted and lay down to sleep: in a
    dream he saw Khaḍir amidst the verdure,[2]
Who said, 'Hark, you have held back from praising God:
    why do you repent of calling unto Him?'
He answered, 'No "Here am I" is coming to me in
    response: I fear that I am turned away from
    the Door.'
Said Khaḍir, 'Nay; God saith: That "Allah" of thine is
    My "Here am I," and that supplication and grief
And ardour of thine is My messenger to thee. Thy fear
    and love are the noose to catch My Favour.
Beneath every "O Lord" of thine is many a "Here am I"
    from Me.'

RAN

1 *Math.* III, 189. Selfless prayer arises from the presence of God in
the heart and is answered before it is uttered.
2 The mysterious holy personage known by the name of Khaḍir
assumes many forms in Moslem legend. See the *Encyclopaedia of
Islam.* 'Verdure' in this verse alludes to his name, literally 'the green
man', and his association with spiritual life and growth.

SOLOMON'S CROOKED CROWN

Solomon was busy judging others,
when it was his personal thoughts
that were disrupting the community.

His crown slid crooked on his head.
He put it straight, but the crown went
awry again. Eight times this happened.

Finally he began to talk to his headpiece.
'Why do you keep tilting over my eyes?'

'I have to. When your power loses compassion,
I have to show what such a condition looks like.'

Immediately Solomon recognized the truth.
He knelt and asked forgiveness.
The crown centered itself on his crown.

When something goes wrong, accuse yourself first.
Even the wisdom of Plato or Solomon
can wobble and go blind.

Listen when your crown reminds you
of what makes you cold toward others,
as you pamper the greedy energy inside.

CB

THE EVIL IN OURSELVES[1]

The Lion took the Hare with him: they ran together
    to the well and looked in.
The Lion saw his own image: from the water appeared
    the form of a lion with a plump hare beside him.
No sooner did he espy his enemy than he left the Hare
    and sprang into the well.
He fell into the pit which he had dug: his iniquity
    recoiled on his own head.

O Reader, how many an evil that you see in others is
    but your own nature reflected in them!
In them appears all that *you* are – your hypocrisy,
    iniquity, and insolence.
You do not see clearly the evil in yourself; else you
    would hate yourself with all your soul.

1 *Math.* I, 1306. In Rūmī's version of this Indian fable, the carnal
self (*nafs*) is represented as the lion who was lured by a hare to the
mouth of a deep well where, mistaking his own reflexion for a
hated rival, he sprang in and perished miserably. So-called evil is
an illusion arising from the diversity of Divine Attributes – Beauty
and Majesty, Mercy and Wrath, etc. – reflected in human nature,
and only our egoism prevents us from seeing the 'soul of goodness'
everywhere. So far as evil exists in us, its source is the unreal 'self'
(*nafs*) by which we are separated from God. Purge the heart of 'self',
and evil disappears.

Like the Lion who sprang at his image in the water,
    you are only hurting yourself, O foolish man.
When you reach the bottom of the well of your own
    nature, then you will know that the wickedness is
    in *you.*

RAN

THE BLIND FOLLOWER[1]

The parrot looking in the mirror sees
Itself, but not its teacher hid behind,
And learns the speech of Man, the while it thinks
A bird of its own sort is talking to it.[2]

So the disciple full of egoism
Sees nothing in the Shaykh except himself.
The Universal Reason eloquent
Behind the mirror of the Shaykh's discourse –
The Spirit which is the mystery of Man –
He cannot see. Words mimicked, learned by rote,
'Tis all. A parrot he, no bosom-friend!

RAN

---

1 *Math.* V, 1430.
2 Parrots in the East are trained to talk by means of a mirror, behind
which is a curtain. Allegorically the 'mirror' is the holy man, who
serves as a medium between the 'parrot', *i.e.* the disciple, and God,
the invisible Speaker and Teacher.

THE SUFI IN THE ORCHARD

A certain Sufi in quest of revelation was meditating
mystic-wise in an orchard, his face resting on his chin.
Presently he sank down deep into himself.
An interfering busybody, supposing him to be asleep,
cried out at him in disgust.

'Why are you slumbering? Consider rather the
vines. Behold the trees, the Divine marks, the greens!
Heed God's command, "So behold"; turn your face
towards these marks of God's mercy!'

'Its marks are within the heart, father of vanity!' the
Sufi replied. 'The outward things are but marks of the
marks.'

The real orchards and green pastures reside within
the depths of the soul; their outward show is as a
reflexion seen in running waters. Only the phantom of
the orchard appears in the water; the phantom quivers
because of the water's subtlety.

AJA

THE TRUTH WITHIN US[1]

'Twas a fair orchard, full of trees and fruit
And vines and greenery. A Ṣūfī there
Sat with eyes closed, his head upon his knee,
Sunk deep in meditation mystical.
'Why,' asked another, 'dost thou not behold
These Signs of God the Merciful displayed
Around thee, which He bids us contemplate?'
'The signs,' he answered, 'I behold within;
Without is naught but symbols of the Signs.'

What is all beauty in the world? The image,
Like quivering boughs reflected in a stream,
Of that eternal Orchard which abides
Unwithered in the hearts of Perfect Men.

RAN

---

1 *Math.* IV, 1358. An early parallel occurs in the legend of Rābi'ah al-'Adawiyyah. One day in spring-time she entered her house and bowed her head. 'Come out,' said the woman-servant, 'and behold what God hath made.' Rābi'ah answered, 'Come in and behold the Maker.'

THE TREASURE-SEEKER[1]

He was engaged in this prayer when a Voice came
    from Heaven, saying,
'You were told to put the arrow to the bow; but who
    told you to shoot with all your might?
Self-conceit caused you to raise the bow aloft and
    display your skill in archery.
You must put the arrow to the bow, but do not draw
    to the full extent of your power.
Where the arrow falls, dig and search! Trust not in
    strength, seek the treasure by means of piteous
    supplication.'

That which is real is nearer than the neck-artery, and
    you have shot the arrow of thought far afield.[2]
The philosopher kills himself with thinking. Let him
    run on: his back is turned to the treasure.

---

1 *Math.* VI, 2347. A dervish dreamed that a Voice from Heaven bade
him go to the shop of a certain stationer, where he would find a scroll
containing the clue to a hidden treasure. On awaking, he went to the
shop and, having found the scroll, read it with care, followed the
directions exactly, and persevered in the quest for a long time, but all
his efforts were unavailing till he gave up hope and besought God to
help him.
2 'Nearer than the neck-artery.' See *Qur'ān* L, 15.

Most of those destined for Paradise are simpletons, so
    that they escape from the mischief of philosophy.[3]
While the clever ones are pleased with the device, the
    simple ones rest, like babes, in the bosom of the
    Deviser.

RAN

---

3 For the meaning of simpleton (*ablah*) in this well-known Ḥadīth,
cf. Epistle to the Romans, XV, 19: 'wise unto that which is good and
simple unto that which is evil.' 'Their foolishness,' says Sulṭān Walad,
'is the highest wisdom: knowing nought of any but the Beloved, of
Him they are extremely conscious and aware.'

GNATS INSIDE THE WIND

Some gnats come from the grass to speak with Solomon.

'O Solomon, you are the champion of the oppressed.
You give justice to the little guys, and they don't get
any littler than us! We are tiny metaphors
for frailty. Can you defend us?'

'Who has mistreated you?'

'Our complaint is against the wind.'

'Well,' says Solomon, 'you have pretty voices,
you gnats, but remember, a judge cannot listen
to just one side. I must hear both litigants.'

'Of course,' agree the gnats.

'Summon the East Wind!' calls out Solomon,
and the wind arrives almost immediately.

What happened to the gnat plaintiffs? Gone.

Such is the way of every seeker who comes to complain
at the High Court. When the presence of God arrives,
where are the seekers? First there's dying,
then union, like gnats inside the wind.

CB

98

THE FAR MOSQUE

The place that Solomon made to worship in,
called the Far Mosque, is not built of earth
and water and stone, but of intention and wisdom
and mystical conversation and compassionate action.

Every part of it is intelligence and responsive
to every other. The carpet bows to the broom.
The door knocker and the door swing together
like musicians. This heart sanctuary *does*
exist, but it can't be described. Why try!

Solomon goes there every morning and gives guidance
with words, with musical harmonies, and in actions,
which are the deepest teaching. A prince is just
a conceit until he *does* something with generosity.

CB

THE MONK WHO SEARCHED FOR A MAN

A monk ran about the bazaar in the daytime with a candle in his hand, his heart full of love and passionate ardour.

'Hi, you!' a busybody shouted to him. 'What are you searching for from shop to shop? Why are you going round searching with a candle in broad daylight? What's the joke?'

'I am searching everywhere for a man,' said the monk. 'A man living by the life of that Breath. Is there a man?'

'A man? Why, the bazaar is full,' the other replied. 'There are men all right, noble sage.'

'Ah,' said the monk, 'but the man I want is one who proves himself a man on the two-way road, in the way of wrath, and at the moment of desire. Where is the man who is truly a man at the time of wrath and the time of lust? In quest of such a man I am running from street to street. Where in all the world is a man who is a true man in these two estates, that I may dedicate my life to him?'

AJA

THE THIEF IN THE ORCHARD

A man climbed a tree in an orchard and began very thievishly to shake down the fruit. The owner of the orchard happened along just then.

'Hey, you scoundrel!' he shouted. 'Aren't you ashamed before God? What are you doing?'

'If,' the thief retorted, 'the servant of God eats from the orchard of God the dates God has given him, why do you vulgarly blame him? Niggardliness at the table of so rich a Master?'

'Aibak!' the owner called his servant. 'Bring that rope here, and I'll give a proper answer to our fine friend.'

With that he promptly tied him tightly to the tree and set about him with a stick, beating him on the back and legs.

'At least have some shame before God!' cried the thief. 'You're killing this innocent miserably.'

'With the stick of God,' the owner replied, 'this servant of God is thrashing the back of another servant of God. The stick is God's, the back and sides are God's. I am the slave and instrument of His command.'

'Sly you are!' the thief conceded. 'I repent. I'm no longer a predestinarian. Free-will it is, free-will, free-will!'

A J A

FINE FEATHERS[1]

'Needs must I tear them out,' the peacock cried,
'These gorgeous plumes which only tempt my pride.'

Of all his talents let the fool beware:
Mad for the bait, he never sees the snare.
Harness to fear of God thy strength and skill,
Else there's no bane so deadly as free-will.

RAN

---

1 *Math.* V, 648. Human powers and capacities, unless devoted to the
service of God, breed false confidence and bring disaster. The moral,
however, is not that we must deliberately throw away the weapons
without which the victory over ourselves cannot be won, but that we
should beware of relying on them and taking credit for any success
they enable us to achieve.

THE FOAL THAT WOULD NOT DRINK

A foal and a mare were once drinking the water.
All the time the stablemen were coaxing the horses,
'Come on now, drink!'

The foal heard their clucking. It lifted its head and
refused to drink.

'Foal, why do you all the time refuse to drink this
water?' asked the mare.

'That mob keep on clucking,' replied the foal. 'Their
sudden noise terrifies me, so that my heart trembles
and jumps about. It is the suddenness of the sound
that makes me afraid.'

'Ever since the world existed,' said the mare, 'there
have been busybodies like these on the earth.'

Attend to your own business, my good man; the
busybodies will soon be plucking out their beards in
vexation.

AJA

AN EMPTY GARLIC

You miss the garden,
because you want a small fig from a random tree.
You don't meet the beautiful woman.
You're joking with an old crone.
It makes me want to cry how she detains you,
stinking mouthed, with a hundred talons,
putting her head over the roof edge to call down,
tasteless fig, fold over fold, empty
as dry-rotten garlic.

She has you tight by the belt,
even though there's no flower and no milk
inside her body.
Death will open your eyes
to what her face is: leather spine
of a black lizard. No more advice.

Let yourself be silently drawn
by the stronger pull of what you really love.

CB

THE CAMEL, THE OX AND THE RAM

A camel, an ox and a ram were going along the way when they came upon a bunch of grass lying on the road in front of them.

'If we divide this up,' the ram said, 'for a certainty not one of us will get his fill of it. But whichever of us has lived the longest has the best right to this fodder; let him eat it; for Muhammad set an example for all to follow, to give priority to one's elders. Comrades, since such a piece of luck has come our way, let each of us declare his age. The oldest has the best right; the rest keep silent. As for myself,' the ram concluded, 'I shared the same pasture in those long ago times with the ram that Abraham sacrificed for Ishmael.'

'I am the most ancient in years,' said the ox. 'I was paired with the ox that Adam yoked. I am the yoke-fellow of the very ox with which Adam, the ancestor of mankind, ploughed the earth in the season of sowing.'

The camel listened to the ox and the ram in amazement. He lifted his head and seized the grass; without further ado, the Bactrian camel raised up in the air that bunch of green barley.

'I don't need to rely on age,' he grunted. 'Not with such a body and such a high neck.'

AJA

THE MAN WHO STOLE A SNAKE,
ON THE ANSWER TO PRAYER

A thief once stole a snake from a snake-catcher, and in
his folly accounted it a rich prize. The snake-catcher
escaped from the bite of the snake; the man who had
stolen his snake was killed by it most miserably.
The snake-catcher saw him, and recognized him.

'Well, well,' he remarked. 'My snake has robbed him
of life. My soul was begging and beseeching God that
I might find the thief and take my snake back from
him. Thanks be to God that my prayer was rejected.
I supposed it to be a loss, and it turned out a gain.'

Many a prayer there is that involves loss and
destruction, which the Holy God in his great goodness
does not hear.

AJA

GALEN AND THE MADMAN

Galen said to his companions, 'One of you administer to me such-and-such a drug.'

'Learned professor,' one of them replied, 'the drug you name is prescribed in cases of lunacy. Far be this from your powerful mind! Do not speak of it again!'

'A lunatic,' Galen explained, 'turned his face to me, looked into my face agreeably for a while, winked at me, and pulled me by the sleeve. If I had not been to some extent his congener, how would that ugly creature have turned his face towards me? How would he have approached me, had he not seen in me one of his own kind? How would he have flung himself upon one of another kind?'

When two people rub shoulders together, without a doubt there is something common between them. Does a bird fly save with its own kind?

The company of the uncongenial is the grave and the tomb.

AJA

OMAR AND THE MAN WHO THOUGHT HE SAW THE NEW MOON

Omar was caliph; the month of the fast had come round. A crowd of people ran to the top of a hill to draw a good omen from the sight of the crescent moon.

'See, Omar!' cried one. 'The new moon!'

Omar did not see any moon in the sky.

'This moon,' he remarked to the man, 'has risen from your imagination. Otherwise, how is it that I do not see the pure crescent, seeing that I am a better scanner of the skies than you? Wet your hand,' he went on, 'and rub it on your eyebrow, then take another look at the new moon.'

The man wetted his eyebrow, and no more saw the moon.

'The moon is no more, King!' he cried. 'It has vanished.'

'Yes,' commented Omar. 'The hair of your eyebrow became a bow and shot at you an arrow of surmise.'

One hair through becoming crooked had waylaid him completely, so that he falsely claimed boastfully to have seen the moon.

If one crooked hair can veil the whole sky, how will it be if all your parts are crooked?

AJA

RED SHIRT

Has anyone seen the boy who used to come here?
Round-faced troublemaker, quick to find a joke,
slow to be serious. Red shirt,
perfect coordination, sly,
strong muscles, with things always in his pocket:
    reed flute
ivory pick, polished and ready for his talent.
You know that one.

Have you heard stories about him?
Pharaoh and the whole Egyptian world
collapsed for such a Joseph.
I'd gladly spend years getting word
of him, even third or fourth-hand.

CB

THE GRAMMARIAN AND THE BOATMAN

A grammarian once embarked in a boat. Turning to the boatman with a self-satisfied air he asked him:

'Have you ever studied grammar?'

'No,' replied the boatman.

'Then half your life has gone to waste,' the grammarian said.

The boatman thereupon felt very depressed, but he answered him nothing for the moment. Presently the wind tossed the boat into a whirlpool. The boatman shouted to the grammarian:

'Do you know how to swim?'

'No,' the grammarian replied, 'my well-spoken, handsome fellow.'

'In that case, grammarian,' the boatman remarked, 'the whole of your life has gone to waste, for the boat is sinking in these whirlpools.'

You may be the greatest scholar in the world in your time, but consider, my friend, how the world passes away – and time!

AJA

THE THREE BROTHERS AND THE
CHINESE PRINCESS

There was a king who had three
equally accomplished sons.

Each was generous and wise, and fiercely
decisive when the need arose.

They stood like three strongly burning candles
before their father, ready to set out on a journey
to distant parts of his kingdom to see
if they were being administered fairly and well.

Each kissed the king's hand as a sign
of farewell and obedience.

'Go wherever you are drawn to go,' said the king,
'and dance on your way.
                    You are protected.
I only warn you not to enter one particular
castle, the one called *The Fortress
That Takes Away Clarity.*

That castle has a gallery of beautiful pictures
which causes great difficulty for the royal family.
It's like the chamber Zuleikha decorated to trap Joseph,

where her picture was everywhere.

He could not avoid
looking at her. Stay away from that one place.'

Of course, as it happens, the three princes
were obsessed with seeing *that* castle, and in spite
of their father's admonition they went
into it.

It had five gates facing the land and five
facing the ocean, as the five external senses
take in the color and perfume of phenomena
and the five inner senses open onto the mystery.

The thousands of pictures there made the princes
restless. They wandered the hallways drunkenly,
until they came,

all three at the same time,
to stand before a particular portrait,

a woman's face.
They fell hopelessly in love. 'This is what our father
warned us of. We thought we were strong enough
to resist anything, as one who has phthisis
thinks he's well enough to go on,

but we're not!
Who is this?'

A wise sheikh revealed to them, 'She
is the Chinese princess, the hidden one.

The Chinese king has concealed her as the spirit
is wrapped in an embryo. No one may come
into her presence.
                        Birds are not even allowed
to fly over her roof. No one can figure a way in.
She can't be won by contriving. Give up on that!'

The princes put their heads together anyway,
comrades in one sighing passion.

The oldest said, 'We've always been bold
when we gave counsel to others, but look at us!
We used to say, *Patience is the key*, but the rules
we made for others are no help now. We advised, *Laugh!*
Why are we so quiet? Where is our strength?'
                                    In despair
they set out for China, not with any hope for a union
with the princess, but just to be closer to her.

They left everything and went toward the hidden
      beloved.
They lived disguised in the capital, trying
to devise some way into the palace.
Finally the eldest, 'I can't wait like this.
I don't want to live if I have to live separated
from the beloved. This is the one
I've been beating the drum for my entire life.

What does a duck care about a shipwreck?
Just the duck's feet in ocean water is ship enough.
My soul and my body are married to this boasting.
I am dreaming but I'm not asleep.
I brag but I do not lie.

                I'm a candle.
Pass the knife through my neck a hundred times,
I'll burn just as brightly.

                     The haystack of my existence
has caught on both sides. Let it burn all night
down to nothing.

                On the road the moon gives
all the light I need. I'm going to confront the king
with my desire.'

                  His brothers tried to persuade him
not to, but they couldn't. He sprang up
and came staggering into the presence of the Chinese
king, who knew what was happening, though
he kept silent.

                That king was *inside* the three
brothers, but he pretended to be unfamiliar
with them.

                The fire under the kettle is the appearance.
The boiling water is the reality.

                     The beloved
is in your veins though he or she may *seem*
to have a form outside you.

The prince knelt
and kissed the king's feet, and stayed there,
bowed down.

'This young man will have everything
he seeks, and twenty times that which he left
behind. He gambled and flung off his robe
in ecstasy. Such love is worth a thousand robes.
This one is an ambassador from that love,
and he is doing his work well.'

The prince heard this
and could not speak, but his soul spoke constantly
with that soul. The prince thought, '*This* is
reality, this waking, this melting away.'

He stayed bowed down with the king a long time,
cooking. 'Execution is one thing,

but I am being executed
again and again every moment! Poor in wealth,
but rich in lives to sacrifice.

No one can play
the game of love with just one head!'

This joyful waiting
consumed the prince. The *form* of the beloved
left his mind and he found union.

'The clothes of the body were sweet silk,
but this nakedness is sweeter.'

This subject can go
no further. What comes next must stay hidden.

One rides
to the ocean on horseback, but after that
the wooden horse of mystical silence
must carry you.

When that boat sinks,
you are the fish, neither silent nor speaking,
a marvel with no name.

So the oldest brother died,
and the middle brother came to the funeral.

'What's this?
A fish from the same sea!' mused the king.
The chamberlain
called out, 'A son of the same father, the brother
next in age to the deceased.'

The king, 'Yes, a keepsake
from that one to me.'

So the sublime kindnesses
descended again, and the courtyard seemed split apart
like a pomegranate laughing, with all the forms
of the universe opening their tent flaps,
new creations every second.

He had read about such
revelations in books. Now it was his. He kept saying,
'Is there more? Is there more?' Fed from the king's
nature,

he felt a satisfaction he'd never felt before,
and then there came a pride.

'Am I not also a king,
the son of a king? Why is this one controlling *me*?
I should open my own shop, independent of him.'

The king thought, 'I give you pure light,
and you throw dirt in my face!'
The middle brother
suddenly realized what he had inwardly done,
but it was too late.

His magnificence
was stripped away. No longer a garden peacock,
he flew like a lonely owl in the wilderness,
like Adam plowing an ox far from Eden.

He came to himself
and asked forgiveness, and with his repentance
he combined something else, the deep pain
that comes from losing the union.

This story must be
shortened. After a year when the king came out
of his own self-effacement, he found one arrow missing
from his quiver and the middle brother dead,
shot through the throat.

The king wept, both slayer
and chief mourner. Yet all was well. The middle
brother too

had gone to the beloved through the killing eye
that blasted his conceit.

It was the third brother,
who had been ill up until now,
who received the hand of the princess.

He lived the marriage of form and spirit,
and did absolutely nothing
to deserve it.

CB

QUATRAINS

Light the incense!
You have to burn to be fragrant.
To scent the whole house
You have to burn to the ground.

***

You only need smell the wine
For vision to flame from each void –
Such flames from wine's aroma!
Imagine if you were the wine.

***

Desperation, let me always know
How to welcome you –
And put in your hands the torch
To burn down the house

***

You see through each cloak I wear:
Know if I speak without mouth or language.
The world is drunk on its desire for words:
I am the slave of the Master of silence.

***

I am so close to you I am distant
I am so mingled with you I am apart
I am so open I am hidden
I am so strong I totter

***

In love with him, my soul
Lives the subtlest of passions
Lives like a gypsy –
Each day a different house
Each night under the stars.

***

You're sea; I'm fish.
You're desert; I'm gazelle.
Fill me with your breath, I live on it,
I'm your reed, your reed.

***

I can't know, only you can,
What makes my heart laugh,
This branch of flowers
Shaking in your wind.

***

'You're the soul,' I said, 'You can't leave the body.'
'How can you know the soul,' he said, 'as you know
　　the body?'
'You're the sea of goodness,' I said. 'Silence!' he said
'Love's a jewel you can't hand over like a stone.

***

I groaned; 'Be quiet,' he said.
I was quiet: he said, 'Groan!'
I grew feverish: he said, 'Be calm!'
I grew calm; he said, 'I want you to burn.'

***

I groaned, he burnt me while I groaned
I fell silent, his fire fell on me
He drove me out beyond all limit
I ran inside, he burnt me there

***

Near truth's blaze what are 'doubt' or 'certainty'?
Bitterness dies near the honey of truth.
Doesn't the sun hide its face before his?
What are these small lights that linger?

A H

IF YOU STAY AWAKE

if you stay awake
for an entire night
watch out for a treasure
trying to arrive

you can keep warm
by the secret sun of the night
keeping your eyes open
for the softness of dawn

try it for tonight
challenge your sleepy eyes
do not lay your head down
wait for heavenly alms

night is the bringer of gifts
Moses went on a ten year journey
during a single night
invited by a tree
to watch the fire and light

Mohammed too made his passage
during that holy night
when he heard the glorious voice
when he ascended to the sky

day is to make a living
night is only for love
commoners sleep fast
lovers whisper to God all night

all night long
a voice calls upon you
to wake up
in the precious hours

if you miss
your chance now
your soul will lament
when your body is left behind

NK

ASLEEP TO THE WORLD[1]

Every night Thou dost free our spirits from the body's
      snare and erase all impressions on the tablets
      (of memory).
Our spirits are set free every night from this cage,
      they are done with audience and talk and tale.
At night prisoners forget their prison, at night
      governors forget their power.
There is no sorrow, no thought of gain or loss, no idea
      of this person or that person.
Such is the state of the mystic, even when he is not
      asleep: God saith, '(*Thou wouldst deem them awake*)
      whilst they slept.'[2]
He is asleep, day and night, to the affairs of this world,
      like a pen in the hand of the Lord.[3]
God hath shown forth some part of his state, inasmuch
      as the vulgar too are carried away by sleep:
Their spirits gone into the Wilderness that is beyond
      words, Their souls and bodies at rest.

---

1 *Math.* I, 388.
2 An allusion to the legend of the Seven Sleepers of Ephesus related
in *Qur'ān* XVIII, 8–25.
3 Cf. the Tradition that 'the true believer is between the two fingers
of God the Merciful.' According as God reveals Himself in the aspect
of Majesty (wrath and terror) or Beauty (mercy and love) the
mystic's heart contracts with grief or expands with joy.

Till with a whistle Thou callest them back to the
    snare, bringest them all again to justice and
    judgement.[4]

RAN

4 *i.e.* to their self-conscious life in the present world, which is a court
of Divine justice where mankind are on trial.

REALITY AND APPEARANCE[1]

'Tis light makes colour visible: at night
Red, green, and russet vanish from thy sight.
So to thee light by darkness is made known:
All hid things by their contraries are shown.
Since God hath none, He, seeing all, denies
Himself eternally to mortal eyes.[2]

From the dark jungle as a tiger bright,
Form from the viewless Spirit leaps to light.
When waves of thought from Wisdom's Sea profound
Arose, they clad themselves in speech and sound.
The lovely forms a fleeting sparkle gave,
Then fell and mingled with the falling wave.
So perish all things fair, to re-adorn
The Beauteous One whence all fair things were born.

RAN

1 *Math.* I, 1121. The symbolism of light and colour comes originally
from Plato.
2 Having no object to compare and contrast with God, the mind
cannot apprehend Him: it perceives only the diverse forms in which
He appears.

GOD IN NATURE[1]

The world is frozen: its name is *jamād* (inanimate):
　　jāmid means 'frozen,' O master.
Wait till the rising of the sun of Resurrection, that thou
　　mayst see the movement of the world's body.[2]
Since God hath made Man from dust, it behoves thee
　　to recognize the real nature of every particle of
　　the universe,
That while from this aspect they are dead, from that
　　aspect they are living: silent here, but speaking
　　Yonder.
When He sends them down to our world, the rod of
　　Moses becomes a dragon in regard to us;[3]
The mountains sing with David, iron becomes as wax
　　in his hand;[4]
The wind becomes a carrier for Solomon, the sea
　　understands what God said to Moses concerning it.[5]

1 *Math.* III, 1008.
2 At the Resurrection, *i.e.* when, either here or hereafter, God lets us
see things as they really are, we shall know the material world in its
inward aspect, which is the world of spirit and everlasting life.
3 *Qur'ān* VII, 104 *seqq.*
4 *Qur'ān* XXI, 79; XXXIV, 10.
5 The wind was subject to Solomon (*Qur'ān* XXI, 81) and
transported his throne from one country to another. God said to
Moses, 'Smite the sea with thy rod' (*Qur'ān* XXVI, 63), whereupon it
opened a way for the Israelites but engulfed Pharaoh and his hosts.

The moon obeys the sign given by Mohammed, the
fire (of Nimrod) becomes a garden of roses for
Abraham.[6]
They all cry, 'We are hearing and seeing and
responsive, though to you, the uninitiated,
we are mute.'
Ascend from materiality into the world of spirits,
hearken to the loud voice of the universe;
Then thou wilt know that God is glorified by all
inanimate things: the doubts raised by false
interpreters will not beguile thee.[7]

RAN

6 This verse refers to the splitting of the moon (*Qur'ān* LIV, 1) and
to the miraculous preservation of Abraham (*Qur'ān* XXI, 69).
7 According to the *Qur'ān* (XVII, 46), 'there is not a thing in heaven
or earth but glorifies Him'. While for Ṣūfīs *taṣbīḥ-i jamādāt* is a
Divinely revealed truth as well as a fact of mystical experience,
Moslem rationalistic theologians explain that such praise of God can
only be implicit or indirect: *e.g.* the sight of a mineral or plant may
cause the person contemplating it to cry *subḥān Allāh!*

AMOR AGITAT MOLEM[1]

Love is a boundless ocean, in which the heavens are
      but a flake of foam.

Know that all the wheeling heavens are turned by
      waves of Love: were it not for Love, the world
      would be frozen.

How else would an inorganic thing change into a plant?
      How would vegetive things sacrifice themselves to
      become endowed with (the animal) spirit?

How would (the animal) spirit sacrifice itself for the
      sake of that Breath by the waft whereof a Mary
      was made pregnant?[2]

All of them would be stiff and immovable as ice, not
      flying and seeking like locusts.

Every mote is in love with that Perfection and mounts
      upward like a sapling.

Their silent aspiration is, in effect, a hymn of Glory
      to God.

RAN

1 *Math.* V, 3853.
2 The elect are inspired and regenerated by the Divine Spirit which
was breathed into the Virgin Mary (*Qur'ān* XXI, 91; LXVI, 12).
Cf. *Fīhi mā fīhi*, 22: 'The body is like Mary, and every one of us hath a
Jesus within. If the pains (of love) arise in us, our Jesus will be born.'
This recalls Eckhart's doctrine of the birth of Christ in the soul
(Inge, *Christian Mysticism*, 162 *seq.*) and especially his saying 'The
Father speaks the Word into the soul, and when the "son" is born
every soul becomes Mary.'

IMMEDIATE KNOWLEDGE[1]

Come, recognize that your sensation and imagination
    and understanding are like the reed-cane on
    which children ride.
The spiritual man's knowledge bears him aloft; the
    sensual man's knowledge is a burden.
God hath said, *Like an ass laden with books*: heavy is the
    knowledge that is not inspired by Him;[2]
But if you carry it for no selfish ends, the load will be
    lifted and you will feel delight.[3]
How can you become free without the wine of Him,
    O you who are content with the sign of Him?
From attribute and name what is born? Phantasy;
    but phantasy shows the way to the Truth.[4]
Do you know any name without a reality? Or have you
    ever plucked a rose from R.O.S.E.?[5]

1 *Math.* I, 3445.
2 The quotation is from *Qur'ān* LXII, 5.
3 *i.e.* God will endow you with real knowledge.
4 Although the words denoting Divine Names and Attributes
convey but a shadowy idea (*khayāl*) of His nature, yet the Ṣūfī who
recites them and meditates on their meaning becomes inspired with
love for their object; for every Divine Name (*ism*) is ultimately
identical with the Named (*musammā*) whom it objectifies. Regarded
externally it is only 'the name of a name' and constitutes a 'veil'
(*ḥijāb*) over the essence of the Named.
5 'A rose from R.O.S.E.': in Persian, '*gul* from (the letters) *gāf*
and *lām*'.

You have pronounced the name: go, seek the thing
     named. The moon is in the sky, not in the water.
Would you rise beyond name and letter, make yourself
     entirely pure,
And behold in your own heart all the knowledge of the
     prophets, without book, without learning,
     without preceptor.

RAN

MYSTICS KNOW[1]

Since Wisdom is the true believer's stray camel,[2]
>   he knows it with certainty, from whomsoever he
>   may have heard of it,
And when he finds himself face to face with it, how
>   should there be doubt? How can he mistake?
If you tell a thirsty man – 'Here is a cup of water:
>   drink!' –
Will he reply? – 'This is mere assertion: let me alone,
>   O liar, go away.'
Or suppose a mother cries to her babe, 'Come, I am
>   mother: hark my child!' –
Will it say? – 'Prove this to me, so that I may take
>   comfort in thy milk.'
When in the heart of a people there is spiritual
>   perception, the face and voice of the prophet are
>   as an evidentiary miracle.
When the prophet utters a cry from without, the soul
>   of the people falls to worship within,

---

1 *Math.* II, 3591, a passage illustrating the Platonic doctrine of
anamnesis and the self-evidence of truth revealed in mystical
experience.
2 A saying ascribed to 'Alī. The Faithful seek the knowledge of God
which they possessed in past eternity and recognize it immediately
when found.

Because never in the world will the soul's ear have
    heard a cry of the same kind as his.
That wondrous voice is heard by the soul in exile – the
    voice of God calling, *'Lo, I am nigh.'*[3]

RAN

3 *Qur'ān* II, 182.

THE RELATIVITY OF EVIL[1]

There is no absolute evil in the world: evil is relative.
    Recognize this fact.
In the realm of Time there is nothing that is not a foot
    to one and a fetter to another.
To one a foot, to another a fetter; to one a poison, to
    another sweet and wholesome as sugar.
Snake-venom is life to the snake, but death to man;
    the sea is a garden to sea-creatures, but to the
    creatures of earth a mortal wound.
Zayd, though a single person, may be a devil to one
    and an angel to another:
If you wish him to be kind to you, then look on him
    with a lover's eye.
Do not look on the Beautiful with your own eye:
    behold the Sought with the eye of the seeker.
Nay, borrow sight from Him: look on His face with
    His eye.
God hath said, 'Whoso belongs to Me, I belong to
    him: I am his eye and his hand and his heart.'

1 *Math.* IV, 65.

Everything loathly becomes lovely when it leads you
    to your Beloved.[2]

RAN

---

2 In this and the preceding verse the poet refers to three Traditions.
He who gives himself up entirely to God (in *fanā*) is united with Him
(in *baqā*). 'Paradise is encompassed with things we like not,' *i.e.* we
must pass through tribulations in order to reach it.

THE SOUL OF GOODNESS IN
THINGS EVIL[1]

Fools take false coins because they are like the true.
If in the world no genuine minted coin
Were current, how would forgers pass the false?
Falsehood were nothing unless truth were there,
To make it specious. 'Tis the love of right
Lures men to wrong. Let poison but be mixed
With sugar, they will cram it into their mouths.
Oh, cry not that all creeds are vain! Some scent
Of truth they have, else they would not beguile.
Say not, 'How utterly fantastical!'
No fancy in the world is all untrue.
Amidst the crowd of dervishes hides one,
One true fakir. Search well and thou wilt find!

RAN

---

1 *Math.* II, 2928. Error, falsehood and all evil is relative in so far as
it serves to make truth and goodness manifest and is sought, not for
itself, but only because it is mistaken for good. Cf. the argument of
Socrates (*Meno* 77, tr. Jowett): 'They do not desire the evils, who are
ignorant of their nature, but they desire what they suppose to be
goods although they are really evils; and if they are mistaken, and
suppose the evils to be goods, they really desire goods.'

GOOD WORDS[1]

The mother is always seeking her child: the
    fundamentals pursue the derivatives.
If water is confined in a tank, the wind sucks it up; for
    the wind is an elemental spirit, powerful and free.
It frees the water and wafts it away to its source, little
    by little, so that you cannot see it wafting;
And our soul likewise the breath of our praise steals
    away, little by little, from the prison of this world.
The perfumes of our good words ascend even unto
    Him, ascending from us whither He knoweth.[2]
Our breaths soar up with the choice words, as a gift
    from us, to the abode of everlastingness;
Then comes to us the recompense of our praise, a
    recompense manifold, from God the Merciful;
Then He causes us to seek more good words, so that
    His servant may win more of His Mercy.
Verily the source of our delight in prayer is the Divine
    Love which without rest draws the soul home.

RAN

1 *Math.* I, 878. The 'good words' (*al-kalim al-ṭayyiba*) are the Moslem
profession of faith (*lā ilāha illā 'llāh*) and other expressions of praise
and worship, used in the sense which Ṣūfīs attach to them.
2 Cf. *Qur'ān* XXXV, 11.

THE COMPLETE ARTIST[1]

He is the source of evil, as thou sayest,
Yet evil hurts Him not. To make that evil
Denotes in Him perfection. Hear from me
A parable. The heavenly Artist paints
Beautiful shapes and ugly: in one picture
The loveliest women in the land of Egypt
Gazing on youthful Joseph amorously;
And lo, another scene by the same hand,
Hell-fire and Iblīs with his hideous crew:
Both master-works, created for good ends,
To show His Perfect Wisdom and confound
The sceptics who deny His Mastery.
Could He not evil make, He would lack skill:
Therefore He fashions infidel alike
And Moslem true, that both may witness bear
To Him, and worship One Almighty Lord.[2]

RAN

1 *Math.* II, 2535.
2 While the Divine Beauty and Mercy reflected in the nature of true
believers cause them to worship God for love's sake, infidels are
dominated by His Majesty and Wrath and only against their will
confess themselves to be His slaves (*'ibād*).

AN AWKWARD COMPARISON

This physical world has no two things alike.
Every comparison is awkwardly rough.

You can put a lion next to a man,
but the placing is hazardous to both.

Say the body is like this lamp.
It has to have a wick and oil. Sleep and food.
If it doesn't get those, it will die,
and it's always burning those up, trying to die.

But where is the sun in this comparison?
It rises, and the lamp's light
mixes with the day.
                    Oneness,
which is the reality, cannot be understood
with lamp and sun images. The blurring
of a plural into a unity is wrong.

No image can describe
what of our fathers and mothers,
our grandfathers and grandmothers, remains.

Language does not touch the one
who lives in each of us.

CB

SPIRITUAL CHURNING[1]

Thy truth is concealed in falsehood, like the taste of
    butter in buttermilk.
Thy falsehood is this perishable body; thy truth is the
    lordly spirit.
During many years the buttermilk remains in view,
    while the butter has vanished as though it were
    naught,
Till God send a Messenger, a chosen Servant, to shake
    the buttermilk in the churn –
To shake it with method and skill, and teach me that
    my true self was hidden.[2]
The buttermilk is old: keep it, do not let it go till you
    extract the butter from it.
Turn it deftly to and fro, that it may give up its secret.
The mortal body is a proof of the immortal spirit:
    the maundering of the drunken reveller proves
    the existence of the cupbearer.

RAN

---

1 *Math.* IV, 3030.
2 It is the mission of the Ṣūfī Pīr to develop and bring out the
spiritual qualities latent in his disciple, just as an infant learns to
speak by listening to its mother.

THE NECESSARY FOIL[1]

Privation and defect, wherever seen,
Are mirrors of the beauty of all that is.
The bone-setter, where should he try his skill
But on the broken limb? The tailor where?
Not, surely, on the well-cut finished coat.
Were no base copper in the crucible,
How could the alchemist his craft display?

RAN

---

1 *Math.* I, 3201. The nature of everything is made manifest by
contrast with something else that lacks its qualities. Were there
no appearance of darkness and evil, we should be ignorant of light
and good. To be conscious of deficiency is the first step towards
perfection

TRADITION AND INTUITION[1]

The ear is a go-between, the eye a lover in unison with
the beloved; the eye has the actual bliss, while the
ear has only the words that promise it.[2]
In *hearing* there is a transformation of qualities; in
seeing, a transformation of essence.[3]
If your knowledge of fire has been ascertained from
words alone, seek to be cooked by fire!
There is no intuitive certainty until you burn: if you
desire that certainty, sit down in the fire!
When the ear is subtle, it becomes an eye; otherwise, the
words are enmeshed and cannot reach the heart.[4]

RAN

1 *Math.* II, 858.
2 The ear plays the part of a *dallālah* (professional match-maker),
whose business it is to describe a girl's beauty to the prospective
bridegroom.
3 'Hearing' (*samʿ*), *i.e.* knowledge based on authority, whether oral
or written, can change only the mental and moral qualities of the
hearer or reader: it cannot effect that complete transformation of
the 'self' which is wrought by immediate vision of the Divine. In the
next verses Rūmī contrasts the certainty derived from 'hearing'
(*ʿilmu 'l-yaqīn*) with the certainty gained by seeing (*ʿaynu 'l-yaqīn*)
and realized in actual experience (*ḥaqqu 'l-yaqīn*).
4 The rudiments of spiritual knowledge are received through the
ear, and when these ideas penetrate the heart and are apprehended by
the *oculus cordis*, hearing becomes vision.

SOMEONE DIGGING IN THE GROUND

An eye is meant to see things.
The soul is here for its own joy.
A head has one use: for loving a true love.
Legs: to run after.

Love is for vanishing into the sky. The mind,
for learning what men have done and tried to do.
Mysteries are not to be solved. The eye goes blind
when it only wants to see *why.*

A lover is always accused of something.
But when he finds his love, whatever was lost
in the looking comes back completely changed.
On the way to Mecca, many dangers: thieves,
the blowing sand, only camel's milk to drink.
Still each pilgrim kisses the black stone there
with pure longing, feeling in the surface
the taste of the lips he wants.

This talk is like stamping new coins. They pile up,
while the real work is done outside
by someone digging in the ground.

CB

THE ELEPHANT IN THE DARK, ON THE
RECONCILIATION OF CONTRARIETIES

Some Hindus had brought an elephant for exhibition
and placed it in a dark house. Crowds of people were
going into that dark place to see the beast. Finding
that ocular inspection was impossible, each visitor felt
it with his palm in the darkness.

The palm of one fell on the trunk.

'This creature is like a water-spout,' he said.

The hand of another lighted on the elephant's ear.
To him the beast was evidently like a fan.

Another rubbed against its leg.

'I found the elephant's shape is like a pillar,' he said.

Another laid his hand on its back.

'Certainly this elephant is like a throne,' he said.

The sensual eye is just like the palm of the hand.
The palm has not the means of covering the whole of
the beast.

The eye of the Sea is one thing and the foam
another. Let the foam go, and gaze with the eye of the
Sea. Day and night foam-flecks are flung from the sea;
oh amazing! You behold the foam but not the Sea.
We are like boats dashing together; our eyes are
darkened, yet we are in clear water.

AJA

THE LADDER TO HEAVEN[1]

The worldly sense is the ladder to this world; the
    religious sense is the ladder to Heaven.
Seek the well-being of that sense from the physician;
    beg the well-being of this sense from the man
    beloved of God.[2]
The spiritual way ruins the body and, having ruined it,
    restores it to prosperity:
Ruined the house for the sake of the golden treasure, and
    with that same treasure builds it better than before;[3]
Cut off the water and cleansed the river-bed, then
    caused drinking-water to flow in it;[4]
Cleft the skin and drew out the barb, then made fresh
    skin grow over the wound;
Razed the fortress and took it from the infidel, then
    reared thereon a hundred towers and ramparts.[5]

1 *Math.* I, 303.
2 *i.e.* the saintly healer of souls.
3 The spiritual essence of Man is buried in his earthly nature, as a
treasure beneath the floor of a house.
4 Purification of the heart cannot begin till the 'water' of lust,
passion, and all sensuous ideas has been cut off.
5 Ghazālī likens the body to a fortress in which God has placed the
spirit or rational soul with orders to defend it against the 'infidel',
i.e. the carnal soul. When it is occupied by evil passions, the spirit
must destroy it, expel the invaders, and then rebuild it and make it
impregnable.

Sometimes the action of God appears like this,
  sometimes the contrary: (true) religion is nothing
  but bewilderment.
(I mean) not one bewildered in such wise that his back
  is turned on Him; nay, but one bewildered and
  drowned and drunken with the Beloved.[6]
His face is set towards (devoted to) the Beloved, while
  the other's face is just his own.
Look long on the face of everyone, watch attentively:
  it may be that by doing service (to Ṣūfīs) you will
  come to know the face (of the Saint).
Since many a devil hath the face of Adam, you should
  not put a hand in every hand;
For as the fowler whistles to decoy a bird he is bent on
  catching,
Which hears the note of its mate and comes down
  from the air and finds itself entrapped,
So does a vile man steal the language of dervishes to
  fascinate and deceive one who is simple.
The work of holy men is as light and heat; the work of
  the ungodly is trickery and shamelessness.

RAN

6 The discursive reason, contemplating apparently irreconcilable
forms of Divine action, is bewildered. But the bewilderment (ḥayrat)
of mystics dazzled by nearness to the Light of God must not be
confused with that of religious hypocrites who have lost their way in
a maze of ignorance and error.

LOVE IS RECKLESS

Love is reckless; not reason.
Reason seeks a profit.
Love comes on strong, consuming herself, unabashed.

Yet, in the midst of suffering,
Love proceeds like a millstone,
hard surfaced and straightforward.

Having died to self-interest,
she risks everything and asks for nothing.
Love gambles away every gift God bestows.

Without cause God gave us Being;
without cause, give it back again.
Gambling yourself away is beyond any religion.

Religion seeks grace and favor,
but those who gamble these away are God's favorites,
for they neither put God to the test
nor knock at the door of gain and loss.

KH

FEELING AND THINKING[1]

Some one struck Zayd a hard blow from behind. He
    was about to retaliate,
When his assailant cried, 'Let me ask you a question:
    first answer it, then strike me.
I struck the nape of your neck, and there was the
    sound of a slap. Now I ask you in a friendly way –
"Was the sound caused by my hand or by your neck,
    O pride of the noble?"'
Zayd said, 'The pain I am suffering leaves me no time
    to reflect on this problem.
Ponder it yourself: he who feels the pain cannot think
    of things like this.'

RAN

1 *Math.* III, 1380. An apologue showing the futility of intellectual
speculation in the face of mystical truth.

TENDING TWO SHOPS

Don't run around this world
looking for a hole to hide in.

There are wild beasts in *every* cave!
If you live with mice,
the cat claws will find you.

The only real rest comes
when you're alone with God.

Live in the nowhere that you came from,
even though you have an address here.

That's why you see things in two ways.
Sometimes you look at a person
and see a cynical snake.

Someone else sees a joyful lover,
and you're both right!

Everyone is half and half,
like the black and white ox.

Joseph looked ugly to his brothers,
and most handsome to his father.

You have eyes that see from that nowhere,
and eyes that judge distances,
how high and how low.

You own two shops,
and you run back and forth.

Try to close the one that's a fearful trap,
getting always smaller. Checkmate,
this way. Checkmate that.

Keep open the shop
where you're not selling fishhooks anymore.
You are the free-swimming fish.

CB

THE PARABLE OF THE ANXIOUS COW

Somewhere in the world there is a green island where a sweet-mouthed cow lives alone. She pastures on the entire plain from morn till night, so that she becomes huge and fat, a very choice cow. During the night she does nothing but worry what she will have to eat on the morrow; the anxiety makes her as thin as a hair.

Next morning the field is green again, the green pulse and the corn have sprung waist-high. The cow falls to with the appetite of an ox, chewing and chewing the lot right through till nightfall. Once more she becomes fat and plump and well-rounded, her body is sleek and stout and strong. Night falls, and at once she panics and falls into a fever and wastes away, fearful of finding no fodder.

'What shall I eat tomorrow at mealtime?' she frets.

This is how that cow carries on year after year. She never reflects, 'All these years I have been feeding on this meadow and this pasture. Not for a single day has my provision failed. What is this fear and heart-consuming anxiety of mine?' So when night falls, that fat cow becomes lean again, with 'Alack, my provision is all gone!'

The carnal soul is that cow, and that field is this world, where the soul is for ever made lean by fear for her daily bread.

AJA

THE GREEDY WIFE AND THE CAT

Once there was a respectable married man whose wife was a shrew, a slut and a snaffler. She scoffed whatever he brought home from market, while he had to hold his tongue.

One day our paterfamilias brought home some meat for a guest; it had cost him enormous trouble. The wife devoured the meat, together with the cabobs and the wine. The husband entered the kitchen; she fobbed him off with lies.

'Where's the meat?' the man demanded. 'The guest's arrived. Only the most delicious food should be offered to guests.'

'That cat's eaten the meat,' the woman answered. 'Hurry, buy some more meat if you can!'

'Aibak, bring the scales,' the man called to the servant. 'I want to weigh the cat.'

He weighed the cat. It was half a kilo.

'Crafty woman!' the husband cried. 'The meat weighed half a kilo and a few grammes. The cat's exactly half a kilo. Well, madam, if that's the cat, then where's the meat? Or if that's the meat, then where's the cat?'

AJA

THE DOG IN THE DOORWAY

This is how it is when your animal energies,
the *nafs*, dominate your soul:

You have a piece of fine linen
that you're going to make into a coat
to give to a friend, but someone else uses it
to make a pair of pants. The linen
has no choice in the matter.
It must submit. Or, it's like
someone breaks into your house
and goes to the garden and plants thornbushes.
An ugly humiliation falls over the place.

Or, you've seen a nomad's dog
lying at the tent entrance, with his head
on the threshold and his eyes closed.

Children pull his tail and touch his face,
but he doesn't move. He loves the children's
attention and stays humble within it.

But if a stranger walks by, he'll spring up
ferociously. Now, what if that dog's owner
were not able to control it?

A poor dervish might appear: the dog storms out.
The dervish says, 'I take refuge with God
when the dog of arrogance attacks,'
and the owner has to say, 'So do I!
I'm helpless against this creature
even in my own house!

Just as you can't come close,
I can't go out!'

This is how animal energy becomes monstrous
and ruins your life's freshness and beauty.

Think of taking this dog out to hunt!
You'd be the quarry.

CB

154

THE CARNAL SOUL[1]

Your self (*nafs*) is the mother of all idols: the material
    idol is a snake, but the spiritual idol is a dragon.
'Tis easy to break an idol, very easy; to regard the self
    as easy to subdue is folly, folly.
O son, if you would know the form of the self, read the
    description of Hell with its seven gates.[2]
From the self at every moment issues an act of deceit;
    and in each of those deceits a hundred Pharaohs
    and their hosts are drowned.

RAN

---

1 *Math.* 1, 772.
2 The *nafs* is Hell or a part of Hell; in essence it is one with the Devil.
Therefore Hell, being the nature of the *nafs-i ammārah* (the soul that
commands us to sin), is really subjective. The seven gates or limbos
of Hell typify the vices which lead to perdition (*muhlikat*).

ACTS OF HELPLESSNESS

Here are the miracle-signs you want: that
you cry through the night and get up at dawn, asking,
that in the absence of what you ask for your day
    gets dark,
your neck thin as a spindle, that what you give away
is all you own, that you sacrifice belongings,
sleep, health, your head, that you often
sit down in a fire like aloes wood, and often go out
to meet a blade like a battered helmet.

When acts of helplessness become habitual,
those are the *signs*.

But you run back and forth listening for unusual events,
peering into the faces of travelers.
'Why are you looking at me like a madman?'
I have lost a friend. Please forgive me.

Searching like that does not fail.
There will come a rider who holds you close.
You faint and gibber. The uninitiated say, 'He's faking.'
How could they know?
Water washes over a beached fish, the water
of those signs I just mentioned.

Excuse my wandering.
How can one be orderly with this?
It's like counting leaves in a garden,
along with the song-notes of partridges,
and crows.
        Sometimes organization
and computation become absurd.

CB

MYSTICAL PERCEPTION[1]

The five spiritual senses are linked with one another:
    all the five have grown from one root.[2]
The strength of one invigorates the others: each
    becomes a cupbearer to the rest.
Vision increases the power of speech; the inspired
    speech makes vision more penetrating.
Clairvoyance sharpens every sense, so that perception
    of the unseen becomes familiar to them all.
When one sheep has jumped over a stream, the whole
    flock jump across on each other's heels.
Drive the sheep, thy senses, to pasture; let them
    browse in the verdant meadow of Reality,
That every sense of thine may become an apostle to
    others and lead all their senses into that Paradise;

1 *Math.* II, 3236.
2 The faculties of the soul, corresponding to the five bodily senses, are derived from the Universal Spirit and serve to manifest Divine attributes: they are not separate and distinct but involved in one another. As Edward Carpenter says, 'this (mystical) perception seems to be one in which all the senses unite into one sense'.

And then those senses will tell their secret to thine,
    without words and without conveying either
    literal or metaphorical meanings.[3]

RAN

3 The illumined saint comes as an apostle to shed light on all and
guide them to the Truth. He reads their hearts by pure intuition; his
knowledge is infallible, since it is not communicated to him by words,
which could only be ambiguous and misleading.

THE WORLD OF TIME[1]

Every instant thou art dying and returning. 'This
    world is but a moment,' said the Prophet.
Our thought is an arrow shot by Him: how should it
    stay in the air? It flies back to God.
Every instant the world is being renewed, and we
    unaware of its perpetual change.
Life is ever pouring in afresh, though in the body it
    has the semblance of continuity.[2]
From its swiftness it appears continuous, like the
    spark thou whirlest with thy hand.
Time and duration are phenomena produced by the
    rapidity of Divine Action,
As a firebrand dexterously whirled presents the
    appearance of a long line of fire.

RAN

1 *Math.* I, 1142. The circle of existence begins and ends in a single
point, the Essence of God, which is perceived by us under the form
of extension. To mystics, however, the world is 'but a moment',
i.e. a flash of Divine illumination revealing the One as the Many and
the Many as the One. According to Ṣūfī and other Moslem
metaphysicians, every atom of the Cosmos is continually annihilated
and re-created by the immediate manifestation of Divine Energy.
2 Cf. the saying of Heraclitus, 'To him who enters the same river,
other and still other waters flow.'

QUATRAINS

Hold to what can never be held
So your hands become ghosts:
His hands are clear spirit
How could they hold bone?

***

Pain is the wind his flags unfurl in
The desert his stallions cross and re-cross
Without check or end –
He is my anguish and I am his.

***

If I'd known how savage Love is
I'd have blocked the door of Love's house
Beaten a drum, shouted 'Keep away!'
But I'm in the house ... helpless ...

***

You are the moon: I am your face in a pool.
How could I forget that night you said,
Holding my head, 'I am yours always
Your love came from me; I am your soul.'

***

Of my bones he made the flutes of heaven
And of my skin dried for years
In the wind of longing
This parchment on which he brands his sign.

***

He's fire
I'm oil
This smoke you see around him
Is me

***

All I know is I know nothing –
And knowing that is by his grace.
I dance in the dirt outside his house.
I gaze up at the window lit with him.

***

Everything I am
I draw from you
Battered old bucket
Dipping in your well.

***

For you; this language without words
Kept secret from all other ears ...
Only you hear what I say
Even when I'm shouting in a crowd.

***

I'm a mountain; his voice is this echo
I'm a painting; his brush is always changing me
I'm a lock creaking as his key turns –
You still believe these words are 'mine'?

***

I know nothing any more, except
That knowing you, I know the source
Of Knowing; this fire-spring you pull me in
Sometimes, where 'you' and 'I' burn.

***

He is here, who was never gone
The water never left this river
He is pure musk, I his scent
Can you smell one without the other?

AH

THE MOUSE AND THE CAMEL

A mouse caught hold of a camel's lead rope
in his two forelegs and walked off with it,
imitating the camel drivers.

                        The camel went along,
letting the mouse feel heroic.

                  'Enjoy yourself,'
he thought. 'I have something to teach you, presently.'

They came to the edge of a great river.
The mouse was dumbfounded.

                  'What are you waiting for?
Step forward into the river. You are my leader.
Don't stop here.'

            'I'm afraid of being drowned.'

The camel walked into the water. 'It's only
just above the knee.'

              '*Your* knee! Your knee
is a hundred times over my head!'

              'Well, maybe you shouldn't
be leading a camel. Stay with those like yourself.
A mouse has nothing really to say to a camel.'

'Would you help me get across?'

'Get up on my hump. I am made to take hundreds like
    you across.'

You are not a prophet, but go humbly on the way of
    the prophets,

and you can arrive where they are. Don't try to steer
    the boat.
Don't open a shop by yourself. Listen. Keep silent.
You are not God's mouthpiece. Try to be an ear,
and if you do speak, ask for explanations.

The source of your arrogance and anger is your lust
and the rootedness of that is in your habits.

Someone who makes a habit of eating clay
gets mad when you try to keep him from it.
Being a leader can also be a poisonous habit,
so that when someone questions your authority,
you think, 'He's trying to take over.'
You may respond courteously, but inside you rage.

Always check your inner state
with the lord of your heart.
Copper doesn't know it's copper,
until it's changed to gold.

Your loving doesn't know its majesty,
until it knows its helplessness.

CB

MY SECRET BELOVED

my secret beloved
sent me a secret message

'give me your soul
give me your life

wander like a drifter
go on a journey

walk into this fire with grace
be like a salamander

come into our source of flame
fire transmutes to a rose garden

don't you know that my thorn
is better than the queen of roses

don't you know my heresy
is the essence of spirituality

then surrender your spirit
surrender your life'

oh God i know
a garden is better than a cage

i know a palace
is better than a ruin

but i'm that owl in this world
who loves to live in the ruins of love

i may be that poor wandering soul
but watch all the aspiration and light

watch the glow of God
reflecting from my face

NK

THIS IS LOVE

This is love: to fly to heaven, every moment to rend
a hundred veils;

At first instance, to break away from breath – first
step, to renounce feet;

To disregard this world, to see only that which you
yourself have seen.

I said, 'Heart, congratulations on entering the
circle of lovers,

'On gazing beyond the range of the eye, on running
into the alley of the breasts.'

Whence came this breath, O heart? Whence came
this throbbing, O heart?

Bird, speak the tongue of birds: I can heed your
cipher!

The heart said, 'I was in the factory whilst the
home of water and clay was a-baking.

'I was flying from the workshop whilst the
workshop was being created.

'When I could no more resist, they dragged me;
how shall I tell the manner of that dragging?'

AJA

ONLY YOU

only you
i choose
among the entire world

is it fair
of you
letting me be unhappy

my heart
is a pen
in your hand

it is all
up to you
to write me happy or sad

i see only
what you reveal
and live as you say

all my feelings
have the color
you desire to paint

from the beginning
to the end
no one but you

please make
my future
better than the past

when you hide
i change
to a Godless person

and when you
appear
i find my faith

don't expect
to find any more in me
than what you give

don't search for
hidden pockets because
i've shown you that
all i have
is all you gave.

NK

YOU ARE MY LIFE

You are my life, you are my life, my life; you are my
own, you are my own, my own.

You are my king, worthy of my passion; you are my
candy, worthy of my teeth.

You are my light; dwell within these eyes of mine,
O my eyes and fountain of life!

When the rose beheld you, it said to the lily, 'My
cypress tree came to my rose garden.'

Say, how are you in respect to two scattered things!
your hair, and my distracted state?

The rope of your hair is my shackle, the well of
your chin is my prison.

Where are you going, drunk, shaking your hands?
Come to me, my laughing rose!

AJA

TALKING THROUGH THE DOOR

You said, 'Who's at the door?'
    I said, 'Your slave.'

You said, 'What do you want?'
    'To see you and bow.'

'How long will you wait?'
    'Until you call.'

'How long will you cook?'
    'Till the Resurrection.'

We talked through the door. I claimed
a great love and that I had given up
what the world gives to be in that love.

You said, 'Such claims require a witness.'
    I said, 'This longing, these tears.'

You said, 'Discredited witnesses.'
    I said, 'Surely not!'

You said, 'Who did you come with?'
    'The majestic imagination you gave me.'

'*Why* did you come?'
　　'The musk of your wine was in the air.'

'What is your intention?'
　　'Friendship.'

'What do you want from me?'
　　'Grace.'

Then you asked, 'Where have you been
most comfortable?'
　　'In the palace.'

'What did you see there?'
　　'Amazing things.'

'Then why is it so desolate?'
　　'Because all that can be taken away in a second.'

'Who can do that?'
　　'This clear discernment.'

'Where can you live safely then?'
　　'In surrender.'

'What is this giving up?'
    'A peace that saves us.'

'Is there no threat of disaster?'
    'Only what comes in your street,
    inside your love.'

'How do you walk there?'
    'In perfection.'

Now silence. If I told more of this conversation,
those listening would leave themselves.

There would be no door,
no roof or window either!

CB

AS YOUR SWORD

as your sword
comes down on my neck
my eyes
will not turn
from your face

when my mouth
is bandaged shut
and this body
laid in the dirt
my eyes
will not turn
from your face

I ask nothing
nothing of you
but your beauty
    your imperious beauty

DL

SWEEP THE DUST OFF THE SEA

The Beautiful One handed me a broom and said,
'Sweep the dust from the sea!'

then burned the broom in the fireplace and said,
'Give me back my broom.'

Bewildered, I put my head to the ground.
'In real submission there's no longer
even someone to bow.'

'But how?'
'Without hesitation or anything of yourself.'

I bared my neck and said,
'Sever me from myself with Ali's sword.'

But as I was struck, and struck again,
countless heads appeared.

As if I were a lamp, and each head a wick,
flames rose on every side,

countless candle-eyed heads,
a procession spanning East and West.
But what is East or West within placelessness?

Its all a furnace and a bath house.
Your heart is cool; how long will you lie in this
        warm bath house?

Leave the bath house and its stove.
Undress yourself in the inner world
and appreciate the frescoes, the beautiful figures,
colored with the hues of the tulip bed;
look towards the window that lets in the light.

The six directions are the bath house,
and a window opens toward the placeless.
Above it is the beauty of a Sovereign

from whose reflection the earth and the sky
received their color, from Whom soulfulness
has rained down upon the Turk and Zanzibari.

The day is gone, and my story ends.
Night and day are shamed by my beauty's story.

The Sun of Tabriz keeps me
drunk and languishing in this state.

KII

YOU ASK ME

you ask me
who are you and
with such a shaky
existence how can you
fall in love

how do i know
who am i or where i am
how could a single wave
locate itself
in an ocean

you ask me
what am i seeking
above and beyond
the pure light
that i once was

and why am i
imprisoned in this cage
named body and
yet i claim to be
a free bird

how do i know
how i lost my way
i know for sure
i was all straight
before i was
seduced by love

NK

THE WINE OF LOVE

He comes, a Moon whose like the sky ne'er saw, awake
    or dreaming,
Crowned with eternal flame no flood can lay.
Lo, from the flagon of Thy love, O Lord, my soul is
    swimming,
And ruined all my body's house of clay.

When first the Giver of the grape my lonely heart
    befriended,
Wine fired my bosom and my veins filled up;
But when His image all my eye possessed, a voice
    descended:
 'Well done, O sovereign Wine and peerless Cup!'

Love's mighty arm from roof to base each dark abode
    is hewing
Where chinks reluctant catch a golden ray.
My heart, when Love's sea of a sudden burst into its
    viewing,
Leaped headlong in, with 'Find me now who may!'

    As, the sun moving, clouds behind him run,
    All hearts attend thee, O Tabrīz's Sun!

RAN

180

YOU ARE DRUNK

you are drunk
and i'm intoxicated
no one is around
showing us the way home

again and again
i told you
drink less
a cup or two

i know in this city
no one is sober
one is worse than the other
one is frenzied and
the other gone mad

come on my friend
step into the tavern of ruins
taste the sweetness of life
in the company of another friend

here you'll see
at every corner
someone intoxicated
and the cup-bearer
makes her rounds

i went out of my house
a drunkard came to me
someone whose glance
uncovered a hundred
houses in paradise

rocking and rolling
he was a sail
with no anchor but
he was the envy of all those sober ones
remaining on the shore

where are you from i asked
he smiled in mockery and said
one half from the east
one half from the west
one half made of water and earth
one half made of heart and soul
one half staying at the shores and
one half nesting in a pearl

i begged
take me as your friend
i am your next of kin
he said i recognize no kin
among strangers
i left my belongings and

entered this tavern
i only have a chest
full of words
but can't utter
a single one

NK

A GREAT WAGON

When I see your face, the stones start spinning!
You appear; all studying wanders.
I lose my place.

Water turns pearly.
Fire dies down and doesn't destroy.

In your presence I don't want what I thought
I wanted, those three little hanging lamps.

Inside your face the ancient manuscripts
seem like rusty mirrors.

You breathe; new shapes appear,
and the music of a desire as widespread
as Spring begins to move
like a great wagon.
                    Drive slowly.
Some of us walking alongside
are lame!

CB

YOU ARE

you are
a sudden resurrection
an endless bliss
you set a fire
in the meadow
of our dreams

laughing today
you are happy
crashing the prisons
blessing the poor

like God Himself
unveiling the sun
spreading hope
bestowing a quest
being the quest
beginning a beginning
setting the end
filling hearts
arranging minds
giving desires
and filling desires

to make a meager living
is not worth the suffering
i let go of preaching
and fill myself with sweets

i set the paper aside
break my pen
name myself silence
i see the cup-bearer is arriving now

NK

DID I NOT SAY TO YOU

Did I not say to you, 'Go not there, for I am your
friend; in this mirage of annihilation I am the fountain
of life?'

Even though in anger you depart a hundred
thousand years from me, in the end you will come to
me, for I am your goal.

Did I not say to you, 'Be not content with worldly
forms, for I am the fashioner of the tabernacle of your
contentment?'

Did I not say to you, 'I am the sea and you are a
single fish; go not to dry land, for I am your crystal
sea?'

Did I not say to you, 'Go not like birds to the
snare; come, for I am the power of flight and your
wings and feet?'

Did I not say to you, 'They will waylay you and
make you cold, for I am the fire and warmth and heat
of your desire?'

Did I not say to you, 'They will implant in you
ugly qualities so that you will forget that I am the
source of purity to you?'

Did I not say to you, 'Do not say from what
direction the servant's affairs come into order?' I am
the Creator without directions.

If you are the lamp of the heart, know where the road is to the house; and if you are godlike of attribute, know that I am your Master.

AJA

QUATRAINS

Real value comes with madness,
matzub below, scientist above.

Whoever finds love
beneath hurt and grief

disappears into emptiness
with a thousand new disguises.

***

Dance, when you're broken open.
Dance, if you've torn the bandage off.
Dance in the middle of the fighting.
Dance in your blood.
Dance, when you're perfectly free.

***

Don't let your throat tighten
with fear. Take sips of breath
all day and night, before death
closes your mouth.

***

Today, like every other day, we wake up empty
and frightened. Don't open the door to the study
and begin reading. Take down a musical instrument.

Let the beauty we love be what we do.
There are hundreds of ways to kneel and kiss
        the ground.

***

Out beyond ideas of wrongdoing and rightdoing,
there is a field. I'll meet you there.

When the soul lies down in that grass,
the world is too full to talk about.
Ideas, language, even the phrase *each other*
doesn't make any sense.

***

The breeze at dawn has secrets to tell you.
                Don't go back to sleep.
You must ask for what you really want.
                Don't go back to sleep.
People are going back and forth across the doorsill
                where the two worlds touch.
The door is round and open.
                Don't go back to sleep.

***

Some nights stay up till dawn,
as the moon sometimes does for the sun.
Be a full bucket pulled up the dark way
of a well, then lifted out into light.

***

I am so small I can barely be seen.
How can this great love be inside me?

*Look at your eyes. They are small,
but they see enormous things.*

***

The light you give off
did not come from a pelvis.

Your features did not begin in semen.
Don't try to hide inside anger
radiance that cannot be hidden.

***

A secret turning in us
makes the universe turn.
Head unaware of feet,
and feet head. Neither cares.
They keep turning.

***

This moment this love comes to rest in me,
many beings in one being.
In one wheat grain a thousand sheaf stacks.
Inside the needle's eye a turning night of stars.

***

Keep walking, though there's no place to get to.
Don't try to see through the distances.
That's not for human beings. Move within,
but don't move the way fear makes you move.

CB

THE DIVINE FACTORY[1]

The Worker is hidden in the workshop: enter the
    workshop and behold Him!
Inasmuch as the work has woven a veil over the
    Worker, you cannot see Him outside of His
    work.[2]
The Worker dwells in the workshop: none who stays
    outside is aware of Him.
Come, then, into the workshop of Not-being, that you
    may contemplate the work and the Worker
    together.[3]
Pharaoh set his face towards material existence;
    therefore he was blind to God's workshop
And wished to alter and avert that which was
    eternally ordained.

RAN

---

1 *Math.* II, 759.
2 God's work is the actualization of the potential. The worker in the
immaterial world perpetually clothes 'not-being' with His Qualities.
3 By dying to self (*fanā*) the mystic returns, as it were, to his pre-
existent state of 'not-being' as an *'ayn-i thābitah* and realizes the
inseparable unity of the Divine Essence, Attributes, and Actions.

CHICKPEA TO COOK

A chickpea leaps almost over the rim of the pot
where it's being boiled.

'Why are you doing this to me?'

The cook knocks him down with the ladle.

'Don't you try to jump out.
You think I'm torturing you.
I'm giving you flavor,
so you can mix with spices and rice
and be the lovely vitality of a human being.

Remember when you drank rain in the garden.
That was for this.'

Grace first. Sexual pleasure,
then a boiling new life begins,
and the Friend has something good to eat.

Eventually the chickpea
will say to the cook,
                        'Boil me some more.
Hit me with the skimming spoon.
I can't do this by myself.

I'm like an elephant that dreams of gardens
back in Hindustan and doesn't pay attention
to his driver. You're my cook, my driver,
my way into existence. I love your cooking.'

The cook says,
          'I was once like you,
fresh from the ground. Then I boiled in time,
and boiled in the body, two fierce boilings.

My animal soul grew powerful.
I controlled it with practices,
and boiled some more, and boiled
once beyond that,
               and became your teacher.'

CB

THE USES OF TRIBULATION[1]

Look at a chickpea in the pot, how it leaps up when it
    is subjected to the fire.

Whilst it is boiling, it always comes up to the top,
    crying ceaselessly,

'Why are you setting the fire on me? You bought me:
    why are you tormenting me like this?'

The housewife goes on hitting it with the ladle. 'Now,'
    says she, 'boil nicely and don't jump away from
    her who makes the fire.

I boil thee, but not because thou art hateful to me; nay,
    'tis that thou mayst get savour

And become nutriment and mingle with the vital
    spirit: such affliction is no abasement.

When thou wert green and fresh, thou drankest water
    in the garden: that water-drinking was for the
    sake of this fire.

God's mercy is prior to His wrath, to the end that by
    His mercy thou mayst suffer tribulation.[2]

---

1 *Math.* III, 4159. The 'housewife' is the *murshid*, the 'chickpea' the
murīd, and the 'fire' the Ṣūfī discipline of self-mortification.
2 There are Traditions in which God declares that His mercy
precedes or prevails over His wrath. Divine Love brought us into
existence, and its object cannot be realized without purging and
transmuting our fleshly qualities (*ṣifātu 'l-bashariyyah*).

His mercy preceded His wrath in order that the stock-
in-trade, which is existence, should be produced;
For without pleasure flesh and skin do not grow, and
unless they grow, what shall Divine Love
consume?
If, because of that requirement, acts of wrath come to
pass to the end that thou shouldst give up thy
stock-in-trade,
Yet afterwards the Grace of God will justify them,
saying "Now thou art washed clean and hast
jumped out of the river."
Continue, O chickpea, to boil in tribulation until
neither existence nor self remains to thee.
If thou hast been severed from the garden of earth,
yet thou wilt be food in the mouth and enter into
the living.[3]
Be nutriment, energy, thought! Thou wert milky sap:
now be a lion of the jungle!
Thou grewest from God's Attributes in the beginning:
pass again into His Attributes!

3 In this and the following verses, spiritual evolution is symbolized by
the process through which a chickpea, when cooked, eaten, assimilated,
and converted into sperm, loses its vegetable nature, participates in
the animal life of man, ascends to rationality, and eventually returns
to the world of Divine Attributes from which it came.

Thou wert a part of the cloud and the sun and the
       stars: thou wilt become soul and action and
       speech and thought.
The life of the animal arose from the death of the
       plant: hence the injunction, "Slay me, O trusty
       friends," is right.
Since such a victory awaits us after death, the words,
       "Lo, in being slain I live," are true.'[4]

RAN

---

[4] The words 'slay me, O trusty friends' and 'in being slain I live' are
quoted from an Arabic ode by Ḥallāj, the most famous of Ṣūfī
martyrs.

YOU HAVE SEIZED ME BY THE EAR

You have seized me by the ear – whither are you drawing me? Declare what is in your heart, and what your purpose is.

Prince, what cauldron did you cook for me last night? God knows what melancholy madness there is in Love!

Since the ears of heaven and earth and the stars are all in your hand, whither are they going? Even to that place whither you said, 'Come!'

The rest you seized only by one ear, me you seized by two; from the roots of each ear I say, 'Long may you endure!'

When a slave grows old, his master sets him free; when I became old, He enslaved me over again.

Shall not children rise up white of hair at the resurrection? But your resurrection has turned the old men's hair black.

Since you bring the dead to life and make the old men young, I have fallen silent, and occupy myself with prayer.

AJA

ENOUGH WORDS?

How does a part of the world leave the world?
How can wetness leave water?

Don't try to put out a fire
by throwing on more fire!
Don't wash a wound with blood!

No matter how fast you run,
your shadow more than keeps up.
Sometimes, it's in front!

Only full, overhead sun
diminishes your shadow.

But that shadow has been serving you!
What hurts you, blesses you.
Darkness is your candle.
Your boundaries are your quest.

I can explain this, but it would break
the glass cover on your heart,
and there's no fixing that.

You must have shadow and light source both.
Listen, and lay your head under the tree of awe.

When from that tree, feathers and wings sprout
on you, be quieter than a dove.
Don't open your mouth for even a *cooooooo*.

When a frog slips into the water, the snake
cannot get it. Then the frog climbs back out
and croaks, and the snake moves toward him again.

Even if the frog learned to hiss, still the snake
would hear through the hiss the information
he needed, the frog voice underneath.

But if the frog could be completely silent,
then the snake would go back to sleeping,
and the frog could reach the barley.

The soul lives there in the silent breath.

And that grain of barley is such that,
when you put it in the ground,
it grows.
      Are these enough words,
or shall I squeeze more juice from this?
Who am I, my friend?

CB

DIE NOW

Die now, die now, in this Love die; when you have died in this Love, you will all receive new life.

Die now, die now, and do not fear this death, for you will come forth from this earth and seize the heavens.

Die now, die now, and break away from this carnal soul, for this carnal soul is as a chain and you are as prisoners.

Take an axe to dig through the prison; when you have broken the prison you will all be kings and princes.

Die now, die now before the beauteous King; when you have died before the King, you will all be kings and renowned.

Die now, die now, and come forth from this cloud; when you come forth from this cloud, you will all be radiant full moons.

Be silent, be silent; silence is the sign of death; it is because of life that you are fleeing from the silent one.

AJA

REMEMBERED MUSIC[1]

'Tis said, the pipe and lute that charm our ears
Derive their melody from rolling spheres;[2]
But Faith, o'erpassing speculation's bound,
Can see what sweetens every jangled sound.[3]

We, who are parts of Adam, heard with him
The song of angels and of seraphim.
Our memory, though dull and sad, retains
Some echo still of those unearthly strains.

1 *Math.* IV, 733.
2 The well-known theory of Pythagoras is almost a commonplace
in Moslem philosophy and poetry. According to the Pure Brethren
(*Ikhwānu 'l-ṣafā*) of Basra, 'since the celestial spheres revolve and the
planets and stars are moved, it follows that they must have musical
notes and expressions with which God is glorified, delighting the
souls of the angels, just as in the corporeal world our souls listen
with delight to melodies and obtain relief from care and sorrow.
And inasmuch as these melodies are but echoes of heavenly music,
they recall to us the spacious gardens of Paradise and the pleasures
enjoyed by the souls dwelling there; and then our souls long to fly
up thither and rejoin their mates.'
3 Ṣūfīs associate the spiritual influence of music with the pre-
existence of the soul. While listening, they hear again the Voice of
God to which all human souls responded in eternity (*Qur'ān* VII,
171) and the anthems of the Heavenly Host.

Oh, music is the meat of all who love,
Music uplifts the soul to realms above.
The ashes glow, the latent fires increase:
We listen and are fed with joy and peace.

RAN

DO YOU BREAK OUR HARP,
EXALTED ONE

Do you break our harp, exalted one; thousands of other harps are here.

Since we have fallen into the clutches of love, what matters it if we lose harp or reed pipe?

If the whole world's rebeck and harp should be consumed, many a hidden harp there is, my friend;

The twanging and strumming mounts to the skies, even if it does not enter the ears of the deaf.

If the whole world's lamp and candle should flicker out, what cause for sorrow is that, since flint and steel still remain?

Songs are spindrift on the face of the sea; no pearl comes on the surface of the sea;

Yet know that the grace of the spindrift derives from the pearl, the reflection of the reflection of whose gleam is upon us.

Songs are all but a branch of the yearning for union; branch and root are never comparable.

Close your lips, and open the window of the heart; by that way be conversant with the spirits.

AJA

THE FLUTE WEEPS

the flute weeps
to the pacing drum

the drunken camel
rises from its knees
and tugs at the rope of reason

the bird flutters
in the heart's cage
putting out his head
on this side and that

the flood fills
the ancient riverbed
and once again
the riverbanks are green

the falcon hears
the royal drum
and circles seeking
the wrist of the king

the musk deer
smells the lion
and her haunches are trembling

the madmen have seen
the moon in the window;
they are running to the roof
with ladders

somewhere tonight
a dervish cries
      'it was my soul
      in the wine!
      it was my soul!'

DL

EVERYWHERE

everywhere
the aroma of God
begins to arrive

look at these people
not knowing their feet from head
as they begin to arrive

every soul is seeking His soul
every soul parched with thirst
they've all heard the voice
of the quencher of thirst

everyone tastes the love
everyone tastes the milk
anxious to know
from where the real mother
begins to arrive

waiting in fever
wondering ceaselessly
when will that final union
begin to arrive

Moslems and Christians and Jews
raising their hands to the sky
their chanting voices in unison
begin to arrive

how happy is the one
whose heart's ear
hears that special voice
as it begins to arrive

clear your ears my friend
from all impurity
a polluted ear
can never hear the sound
as it begins to arrive

if your eyes are marred
with petty visions
wash them with tears
your teardrops are healers
as they begin to arrive

keep silence
don't rush to finish your poem
the finisher of the poem
the creator of the word
will begin to arrive

NK

I AM

i am
the minstrel of
eternal love
and will play
the song of happiness

when my soul
hears music
and changes to softness
I'll break open
the wine jar's seal

i am in love
with the temple of fire
because i was born
as the prophet
named Khalili Abraham

i am in love
with soul and
wisdom
i am the enemy
of false images

the spring is arriving
it is high time
for action
for the sun and Aries
to get together

my blood is boiling
my heart is on fire and
the winter snow
is melting away
from my body

someone's love
is knocking me out
and pulling me
after itself
very forcefully

though i am
in this
hell and fire
i'm filled with
honey and nectar

though i am
condemned to take
this journey
i'm filled with
the sweetness of going home

now the time has come
my sweetheart
kindly express
what my tongue
can never describe

NK

WHATEVER HAPPENS

whatever happens
to the world around
show me your purpose
show me your source

even if the world
is Godless and in chaos
show me your anchor
show me your love

if there is hunger
if there is famine
show me your harvest
show me your resource

if life is bitter
everywhere snakes everywhere poison
show me your garden
show me your meadow

if the sun and the moon fall
if darkness rules the world
show me your light
show me your flame

if i have no mouth
or tongue to utter
words of your secrets
show me your fountain

i'll keep silence
how can i express
your life when mine
still is untold

NK

IF A TREE COULD MOVE
ON FOOT OR WING

If a tree could move on foot or wing, it would not suffer the pain of the saw or the blows of the axe;

And if the sun did not travel on wing and foot all the night, how would the world be illumined at morning-tide?

If the salt water did not rise from the sea to the sky, whence would the garden be revived by torrent and rain?

When the drop departed from its homeland and returned, it encountered a shell and became a pearl.

Did not Joseph go from his father on a journey, weeping? Did he not on the journey attain felicity and kingdom and victory?

Did not Muṣṭafā go on a journey towards Yathrib, gain sovereignty, and become king of a hundred lands?

And you – if you have no foot, choose to journey into yourself; like a ruby-mine be receptive to a print from the sunbeams.

Make a journey out of self into self, my master, for by such a journey earth became a mine of gold.

Go out of sourness and bitterness towards sweetness, just as a thousand sorts of fruits have escaped out of bitterness.

Seek sweetness from the Sun, the Pride of Tabriz, for every fruit gains comeliness from the light of the sun.

AJA

WHERE EVERYTHING IS MUSIC

Don't worry about saving these songs!
And if one of our instruments breaks,
it doesn't matter.

We have fallen into the place
where everything is music.

The strumming and the flute notes
rise into the atmosphere,
and even if the whole world's harp
should burn up, there will still be
hidden instruments playing.

So the candle flickers and goes out.
We have a piece of flint, and a spark.

This singing art is sea foam.
The graceful movements come from a pearl
somewhere on the ocean floor.

Poems reach up like spindrift and the edge
of driftwood along the beach, wanting!

They derive
from a slow and powerful root
that we can't see.

Stop the words now.
Open the window in the center of your chest,
and let the spirits fly in and out.

CB

THE UNSEEN POWER[1]

We are the flute, our music is all Thine;
We are the mountain echoing only Thee;
Pieces of chess Thou marshallest in line
And movest to defeat or victory;
Lions emblazoned high on flags unfurled –[2]
Thy wind invisible sweeps us through the world.

RAN

1 *Math.* I, 599.
2 This was a sight the poet must often have witnessed during his
residence at Qoniyah. Banners and coins bearing the device of a lion
surmounted by a sun are associated with the Seljūq dynasties of 'Irāq
and Asia Minor.

SONG OF THE REED

Listen to the reed and the tale it tells,
how it sings of separation:
Ever since they cut me from the reed bed,
my wail has caused men and women to weep.
I want a heart torn open with longing
to share the pain of this love.
Whoever has been parted from his source
longs to return to that state of union.
At every gathering I play my lament.
I'm a friend to both happy and sad.
Each befriended me for his own reasons,
yet none searched out the secrets I contain.
My secret is not different than my lament,
yet this is not for the senses to perceive.
The body is not hidden from the soul,
nor is the soul hidden from the body,
and yet the soul is not for everyone to see.
This flute is played with fire, not with wind,
and without this fire you would not exist.
It is the fire of love that inspires the flute.
It is the ferment of love that completes the wine.
The reed is a comfort to all estranged lovers.
Its music tears our veils away. Have you
ever seen a poison or antidote like the reed?
Have you seen a more intimate companion and lover?

It sings of the path of blood;
it relates the passion of Majnun.
Only to the senseless is this sense confided.
Does the tongue have any patron but the ear?
Our days grow more unseasonable,
these days which mix with grief and pain . . .
but if the days that remain are few,
let them go; it doesn't matter. But You, You remain,
for nothing is as pure as You are.
All but the fish quickly have their fill of His water;
and the day is long without His daily bread.
The raw do not understand the state of the ripe,
so my words will be brief.

Break your bonds, be free, my child!
How long will silver and gold enslave you?
If you pour the whole sea into a jug,
will it hold more than one day's store?
The greedy eye, like the jug, is never filled.
Until content, the oyster holds no pearl.
Only one who has been undressed by Love,
is free of defect and desire.
O Gladness, O Love, our partner in trade,
healer of all our ills, our Plato and Galen,
remedy of our pride and our vanity.

With love this earthly body could soar in the air;
the mountain could arise and nimbly dance.
Love gave life to Mount Sinai, O lover.
Sinai was drunk; Moses lost consciousness.
Pressed to the lips of one in harmony with myself,
 I might also tell all that can be told;
but without a common tongue, I am dumb,
even if I have a hundred songs to sing.
When the rose is gone and the garden faded,
you will no longer hear the nightingale's song.
The Beloved is all; the lover just a veil.
The Beloved is living; the lover a dead thing.
If Love withholds its strengthening care,
the lover is left like a bird without wings.
How will I be awake and aware
if the light of the Beloved is absent?
Love wills that this Word be brought forth.
If you find the mirror of the heart dull,
the rust has not been cleared from its face.
O friends, listen to this tale,
the marrow of our inward state.

KH

IF YOU CAN ONLY REFLECT

if you can only reflect
like a clean mirror
you'll be that magical spirit

transmute from a wave
to an ocean
from an abyss
to surpass an angel

your soul and mine
used to be mingled
breathing as one
journeying as one

though you're in the limelight now
you must still kiss a candle
to feel the essence
to feel the light

NK

THE ASCENDING SOUL[1]

I died as mineral and became a plant,
I died as plant and rose to animal,
I died as animal and I was Man.
Why should I fear? When was I less by dying?
Yet once more I shall die as Man, to soar
With angels blest; but even from angelhood
I must pass on: *all except God doth perish.*[2]
When I have sacrificed my angel-soul,
I shall become what no mind e'er conceived.
Oh, let me not exist! for Non-existence
Proclaims in organ tones. 'To him we shall return.'[3]

RAN

1 *Math.* III, 3901.
2 *Qur'ān* XXVIII, 88.
3 *Qur'ān* II, 151.

THE PROGRESS OF MAN[1]

First he appeared in the realm inanimate;
Thence came into the world of plants and lived
The plant-life many a year, nor called to mind
What he had been; then took the onward way
To animal existence, and once more
Remembers naught of that life vegetive,
Save when he feels himself moved with desire

1 *Math.* IV, 3637. The doctrine of soul-development set forth by
Rūmī is not peculiar to him: it appears in Moslem philosophy and
mysticism at a much earlier date and is founded on Aristotle's theory
of the triple nature of the soul as poetically described by Milton
(*Paradise Lost* V, 479 *seqq.*):

> So from the root
> Springs lighter the green stalk, from thence the leaves
> More aery, last the bright consummate flower
> Spirits odorous breathes: flowers and their fruit,
> Man's nourishment, by gradual scale sublimed,
> To vital spirits aspire, to animal,
> To intellectual; give both life and sense,
> Fancy and understanding; whence the Soul
> Reason receives, and Reason is her being.

To complete the parallel, these lines should be read in connexion
with Milton's treatise *De doctrinâ Christianâ*, where he elaborates the
view that 'all creation, inanimate and animate, consists but of diverse
forms or degrees of one and the same original or prime *matter*; which
matter was originally an efflux or emanation out of the very substance
of the One Eternal Spirit' (Masson, *The Poetical Works of John Milton*,
III, 361).

Towards it in the season of sweet flowers,
As babes that seek the breast and know not why.[2]
Again the wise Creator whom thou knowest
Uplifted him from animality
To Man's estate; and so from realm to realm
Advancing, he became intelligent,
Cunning and keen of wit, as he is now.
No memory of his past abides with him,
And from his present soul he shall be changed.

Though he is fallen asleep, God will not leave him
In this forgetfulness. Awakened, he
Will laugh to think what troublous dreams he had,
And wonder how his happy state of being
He could forget and not perceive that all
Those pains and sorrows were the effect of sleep
And guile and vain illusion. So this world
Seems lasting, though 'tis but the sleeper's dream;
Who, when the appointed Day shall dawn, escapes
From dark imaginings that haunted him,
And turns with laughter on his phantom griefs
When he beholds his everlasting home.

RAN

2 The functions of the vegetive soul are growth, assimilation, and
reproduction. Spring flowers and verdure awaken in the animal soul,
which is the 'child' of the vegetive soul, subconscious memories of its
'mother'.

WHERE DID IT ALL GO

where did it all go
the dancing the love and the music
could it be that none was there
or it was but all
went to the vanishing point

it is better not to be skeptic
look at Moses' magic cane
one minute a cane the next a dragon

or was it a dragon first
and as it devoured the world
within its existence
it changed to a cane

every situation is
like an arrow
when it is gone my friend
seek and find it in the target

though a pearl
has stolen a grain of sand
from the nearby shore
a wise diver will seek it out
in the depth of the ocean floor

NK

THE NEGATIVE WAY[1]

In the presence of the drunken Turk, the minstrel
      began to sing of the Covenant made in eternity
      between God and the soul.[2]
'I know not whether Thou art a moon or an idol,
      I know not what Thou desirest of me,
I know not what service to do Thee, whether I should
      keep silence or express Thee in words.
'Tis marvellous that Thou art Nigh unto me; yet
      where am I and where Thou, I know not.'
In this fashion he opened his lips, only to sing 'I know
      not, I know not.'
At last the Turk leaped up in a rage and threatened
      him with an iron mace.

---

1 *Math.* VI, 703.
2 'Minstrel' probably denotes the Perfect Man teaching his disciples
to follow the path of self-negation (*fanā*), not as an end in itself but
because it leads to positive and real union with God (*baqā*). In other
words, mystical 'intoxication' (*sukr*) should be regarded only as a
prelude, and therefore relatively inferior, to 'sobriety' (*saḥw*), in
which the mystic rises from negation of the Many to affirmation of
the One revealed in the Many. This is the true significance of the
Moslem profession of faith, *lā ilāha illā 'llāh*, prefigured by the Primal
Covenant (*mīthāq*) in eternity between God and all human souls: '*He
brought forth from the children of Adam, from their reins, their seed, and
made them testify of themselves, saying, "Am not I your Lord?" They
answered, "Yea, we testify."*' See *Qur'ān* VII, 171.

'You crazy fool!' he cried. 'Tell me something you
    know, and if you don't know, don't talk nonsense.'
'Why all this palaver?' said the minstrel, 'My meaning
    is occult.
Until you deny all else, the affirmation of God escapes
    you: I am denying in order that you may find the
    way to affirm.
I play the tune of negation: when you die death will
    disclose the mystery –
Not the death that takes you into the dark grave, but
    the death whereby you are transmuted and enter
    into the Light.
O Amīr, wield the mace against yourself: shatter
    egoism to pieces!'

RAN

DISSOLVER OF SUGAR

Dissolver of sugar, dissolve me,
if this is the time.
Do it gently with a touch of a hand, or a look.
Every morning I wait at dawn. That's when
it's happened before. Or do it suddenly
like an execution. How else
can I get ready for death?

You breathe without a body like a spark.
You grieve, and I begin to feel lighter.
You keep me away with your arm,
but the keeping away is pulling me in.

CB

THE HEART IS LIKE A GRAIN OF CORN

The heart is like a grain of corn, we are like a mill;
how does the mill know why this turning?

The body is like a stone, and the water its
thoughts; the stone says, 'The water knows what is
toward.'

The water says, 'Ask the miller, for it was he who
flung this water down.'

The miller says to you, 'Bread-eater, if this does not
turn, how shall the crumb-broth be?'

Much business is in the making; silence, ask God,
that He may tell you.

AJA

QUATRAINS

'No-one suffers enough,' he said, 'Be the one
Who suffers everything and comes to me
With nothing but this bowl
Into which I can pour my wine.'

***

Heart, if you can't brave grief, go –
Love's glory's not a small thing.
Soul, come in, if you're fearless:
Shudder, and this is not your house.

***

How many times must I say it?
The madman of reason is the man of wisdom
Follow grief's road to the heart
You'll find in your self thousands of strangers.

***

This heart I believed mine for so long
I can't just 'leave' it, even with friends.
My lover has left me and gone near you –
Keep safe what I kept with so many tears.

***

Sunlight in a filthy street
His absence ringing in my ears
Nothing to show for a lifetime's love
But this broken bowl, these tears.

***

Once you said 'I cannot leave
Anyone who's loved me'
Your disappearance
Remains

***

I live in terror of not dying
Of never being him and always me
This carcass whose words are coins
Rattling in a beggar's tin.

***

When I am sad, I am radiant
When I am broken, content
When I am tranquil and silent as the earth
My cries like thunder tremble heaven.

***

It is he who suffers his absence in me
Who through me cries out to himself.
Love's most strange, most holy mystery –
We are intimate beyond belief.

***

Over all the parchments of Egypt
I've scrawled my cries and hungers.
One hour of love's worth a hundred worlds –
I've thousands of hearts; here, burn them all.

***

Ghostly passions are the most violent.
No-one who does not know this can know
Why I lie down in his desert
For his stallions to trample.

***

Take my soul, now. Send me reeling
Drunkenly out of the world . . .
Everything in me good, but not you –
Destroy. Turn this wood to fire.

AH

DEIFICATION[1]

When a fly is plunged in honey, all the members of
its body are reduced to the same condition, and it does
not move. Similarly the term *istighrāq* (absorption in
God) is applied to one who has no conscious existence
or initiative or movement. Any action that proceeds
from him is not his own. If he is still struggling in the
water, or if he cries out, 'Oh, I am drowning,' he is not
said to be in the state of absorption. This is what is
signified by the words *Ana 'l-Ḥaqq* 'I am God.' People
imagine that it is a presumptuous claim, whereas it is
really a presumptuous claim to say *Ana 'l-'abd* 'I am
the slave of God'; and *Ana 'l-Ḥaqq* 'I am God' is an
expression of great humility. The man who says
Ana 'l-'abd 'I am the slave of God' affirms two
existences, his own and God's, but he that says

---

1 *Fīhi mā fīhi*, 49. When he (the mystic) falls into the dyeing-vat
of *Hū* (the Absolute God), and you say to him, 'Arise,' he cries in
rapture, 'I am the vat: do not blame me.' That 'I am the vat' is the
same as saying 'I am God' (*ana 'l-Ḥaqq*): he has the colour of fire,
albeit he is iron.

> The colour of the iron is naughted in the colour of the fire: the iron
> boasts of its fierceness, though actually it is silent.
> It has become glorified by the colour and nature of the fire: it says,
> 'I am the fire, I am the fire.' *Math* II, 1346.

Ana 'l-Ḥaqq 'I am God' has made himself non-existent
and has given himself up and says 'I am God,'
i.e. 'I am naught, He is all: there is no being but
God's.' This is the extreme of humility and
self-abasement.

RAN

WE CAME WHIRLING

we came whirling
out of nothingness
scattering stars
like dust

the stars made a circle
and in the middle
we dance

the wheel of heaven
circles God
like a mill

if you grab a spoke
it will tear your hand off

turning and turning
it sunders
all attachment

were that wheel not in love
it would cry
       'enough! how long this turning?'

every atom
turns bewildered

beggars circle tables
dogs circle carrion
the lover circles
        his own heart

ashamed,
I circle shame

a ruined water wheel
whichever way I turn
is the river

if that rusty old sky
creaks to a stop
still, still I turn

and it is only God
circling Himself

DL

TWO DISCOURSES (AJA)

I

Someone was saying: Our Master does not utter a word.

I said: Well, it was the thought of me that brought this person to my presence. This thought of me did not speak with him, saying, 'How are you?' or 'How are things with you?' The thought without words drew him hither. If the reality of me draws him without words and transports him to another place, what is so wonderful in that? Words are the shadow of reality and the branch of reality. Since the shadow could draw, how much more the reality!

Words are the pretext. It is the element of congeneity that draws one man to another, not words. If a man should see a hundred thousand miracles and expositions and divine graces, if there is no element of congeneity in him connecting him with the prophet or the saint concerned, then all those phenomena will be profitless. It is that element which keeps him agitated and restless. If there were no element of amber in a straw, the straw would never move towards the amber. This congeneity between them is a hidden and not a visible thing.

It is the thought of a thing that brings a man to that thing. The thought of the garden brings him to the garden, the thought of the shop brings him to the shop.

Within these thoughts, however, is a secret deception. Do you not see how you will go to a certain place and then repent of having done so, saying, 'I thought that it would be good. It was not so'? These thoughts then are like a shroud, and within the shroud someone is hidden. Whenever the thoughts vanish from the scene and the realities appear without the shroud of thought, there is a great commotion. Where such is the case, there remains no trace of regret. When it is the reality that draws you, there is nothing there other than the reality. It would be that same reality which drew you hither.

Upon the day when the secrets are tried.

What occasion is there then for me to speak?

In reality that which draws is a single thing, but it appears to be numerous. Do you not see how a man is possessed by a hundred different desires? 'I want vermicelli,' he says. 'I want ravioli. I want halwa. I want fritters. I want fruit. I want dates.' He enumerates these and names them one by one, but the root of the matter is a single thing: the root is hunger, and that is one. Do you not see how, when he has had his fill of one thing, he says, 'None of these things is necessary'? So it is proved that it was not ten or a hundred things but one thing that drew him.

And their number
We have appointed only as a trial.

This 'number' of creatures is a trial appointed by God. They say, 'This man is one and they are a hundred' – that is, they say the saint is one and mankind are many, a hundred and a thousand. This is a great trial. This view and this thought that makes a man see them as many and him as one is a great trial.

> *And their number*
> *We have appointed only as a trial.*

Which hundred? Which fifty? Which sixty? A people without hands and feet, without mind and soul, quivering like a magic talisman, like quicksilver or mercury – call them if you will sixty or a hundred or a thousand, and this man one, but on the contrary the truth is that they are nothing, whereas he is a thousand and a hundred thousand and thousands of thousands.

> Few in the numbering, many in the charge.

A king had given a single soldier a hundred men's rations of bread. The army protested, but the king said within him, 'The day will come when I will show you, and you will know why I did this.' When the day of battle arrived they all fled from the field, and that soldier alone fought. 'There you are,' the king said. 'It was for this purpose.'

It behoves a man to strip his discriminative faculty of all prejudices and to seek a friend in the Faith. Faith consists in knowing who is one's true friend. When, however, a man has spent his life in the company of people who lack discrimination, his own discriminative faculty becomes feeble and he is unable to recognise that true friend of the Faith.

You have nurtured this substance in which there is no discrimination. Discrimination is that one quality which is hidden in a man. Do you not see that a madman possesses hands and feet but lacks discrimination? Discrimination is that subtle essence which is within you. Day and night you have been occupied with nurturing that physical substance without discrimination. You put forward as a pretext that that subsists through this. Yet this likewise subsists through that. How is it that you have devoted all your energies to looking after the physical substance, and have entirely neglected the subtle essence? Indeed, the physical subsists through the other, whereas the other is by no means dependent upon the physical for its subsistence.

That light which shines abroad through the windows of the eyes and ears and so forth – if those windows did not exist, it would nevertheless shine through other windows. It is just as if you had brought a lamp in front of the sun, saying, 'I see the sun by means of this lamp.' God forbid! If you do not bring the lamp, still the sun will show itself: what need is there of a lamp?

It behoves us not to break off hope of God. Hope is

the head of the road to security. If you do not travel upon that road, at least guard the head of that road. Do not say, 'I have done crooked things'; choose the way of straightness, and no crookedness will remain. Straightness is like the rod of Moses, and those crookednesses are as the tricks of Pharaoh's magicians: when straightness comes, it will swallow up all those tricks. If you have done evil, you have done it to yourself; how should your wickedness reach out to affect God?

> The bird that perched on yonder mount,
>   Then rose into the sky –
> Tell me, what gain was there to count?
>   What lost the mount thereby?

When you become straight, all those crookednesses will disappear. So beware, do not break off hope.

The danger of associating with kings consists not in the fact that you may lose your life: one must lose one's life in the end, whether it be today or tomorrow matters not. The danger arises from the fact that when kings enter upon the scene and the spell of their influence gains strength, converting so to speak into a dragon, the man who keeps company with them and lays claim to their friendship and accepts money from them will inevitably speak in accordance with their wishes. He will receive their evil views with the utmost attention and will not be able to gainsay them.

That is where the danger lies, in that it leads to the detriment of the true faith. When you cultivate their interest, the other interest, which is fundamental to the good life, becomes a stranger to you. The more you proceed in that direction, the more this direction, where the Beloved dwells, turns away from you. The more you make your peace with worldly men, the more the Beloved is angry with you. 'Whosoever assists an oppressor, God gives him power over him': your 'going in his direction' renders you subject to this rule. Once you have gone in that direction, in the end God gives him power over you.

It is a pity to reach the sea, and to be satisfied with a little water or a pitcher-full from the sea. After all there are pearls in the sea, and from the sea myriads of precious things may be produced. What worth is there in taking water? What pride can intelligent men have in that, and what will they have accomplished? Indeed, the world is a mere foam-fleck of that Sea; its water is the very sciences of the saints; where is the Pearl itself? This world is but foam full of floating jetsam; but through the turning about of those waves and the congruous surging of the sea and the constant motion of the billows that foam takes on a certain beauty.

> *Decked out fair to men is the love of lusts —*
> *women, children, heaped-up heaps of gold*

> *and silver, horses of mark, cattle*
> *and tillage. That is the enjoyment of*
> *the present life.*

Since therefore God has called it *decked out fair*, it is not truly beautiful; rather its beauty is a borrowed thing, coming from elsewhere. It is false coin gilded; that is to say, this world which is a fleck of foam is false coin, valueless and without worth, but we have gilded it so that it is *decked out fair to men.*

Man is the astrolabe of God; but it requires an astronomer to know the astrolabe. If a vegetable-seller or a greengrocer should possess the astrolabe, what benefit would he derive from it? With that astrolabe what would he know of the movements of the circling heavens and the stations of the planets, their influences, transits and so forth? But in the hands of the astronomer the astrolabe is of great benefit, for 'He who knows himself knows his Lord.'

Just as this copper astrolabe is the mirror of the heavens, so the human being – *We have honoured the Children of Adam* – is the astrolabe of God. When God causes a man to have knowledge of Him and to know Him and to be familiar with Him, through the astrolabe of his own being he beholds moment by moment and flash by flash the manifestation of God and His infinite beauty, and that beauty is never absent from his mirror.

God has servants who cloak themselves in wisdom and gnosis and grace; though other men have not the vision to behold them truly, yet out of the excess of jealousy these servants cloak themselves, even as Mutanabbī says:

Figured silks they wore, not their bodies to beautify
But to guard their beauty against the lustful eye.

II

We are like a bowl on the surface of the water. The movement of the bowl on the surface of the water is controlled not by the bowl but by the water.

Someone said: This statement is of general application. But some people know that they are on the surface of the water, whereas some do not know.

The Master said: If the statement were of general application, then the particular specification that 'The heart of the believer is between two fingers of the All-Merciful' would not be correct. God also said:

The All-Merciful has taught the Koran.

It cannot be said that this is a general statement. God taught all sciences so what is this particularization of the Koran? Similarly:

Who created the heavens and the earth.

What is this particularization of the heavens and the earth, since He created all things in general? Undoubtedly all bowls travel on the surface of the water of Omnipotence and the Divine Will. But it is unmannerly to relate to It a despicable thing, such as 'O Creator of dung and farting and wind-breaking'; one only says, 'O Creator of the heavens' and 'O Creator of the minds.' So this particularization has its significance; though the statement is general, yet the particularization of a thing is an indication of the choiceness of that thing.

The upshot is, that the bowl travels on the surface of the water. The water carries one bowl in such a manner that every bowl gazes upon that bowl. The water carries another bowl in such a manner that every bowl runs away from that bowl instinctively and is ashamed of it. The water inspires them to run away and implants in them the power to run away, so that they say, 'O God, take us farther away from it'; whilst in the former case they say, 'O God, bring us nearer to it.'

The person who regards the situation as general says, 'From the standpoint of subjection, both kinds of bowl are equally subject to the water.' In reply one may say, 'If you only saw the grace and beauty and pretty sauntering of this bowl on the water, you would not have had such care for that general attribute.' In the same way a beloved person is a co-partner with all dungs and every manner of filth from the standpoint of existing. But it would never occur to the lover to say, 'My beloved is a co-partner with all manner of filth in the general description that both are bodies contained in a certain space and comprised in the six directions, created in time and subject to decay' and the rest of the general descriptions. He would never apply these terms to the beloved; and anyone who described the beloved in this general manner he would take as an enemy and deem his particular devil.

Since therefore you find it in you to regard that general attribute, not being worthy to look upon our particular beauty, it is not proper to dispute with you; for our disputations are commingled with beauty, and it is wrong to disclose beauty to those who are not worthy of it. 'Impart not wisdom to those not meet for it, lest you do wisdom wrong; and withhold it not from those meet to receive it, lest you do them wrong.'

This is the science of speculation, it is not the science of disputation. Roses and fruit-blossoms do not bloom in the autumn, for that would be disputation; that is, it would be confronting and competing with the opponent autumn. It is not in the nature of the rose to confront autumn. If the regard of the sun has done its work, the rose comes out in an equable and just atmosphere; otherwise, it draws in its head and retires within its stem. The autumn says to it, 'If you are not a barren branch, confront me, if you are a man!' The rose says, 'In your presence I am a barren branch and a coward. Say whatever you will!'

> O monarch of all truthful men,
> How think you me a hypocrite?
> With living men I am alive,
> And with the dead as dead I sit.

You, who are Bahā' al-Dīn – if some old crone without any teeth, her face all wrinkles like the back of a lizard, should come and say, 'If you are a man and a true youth, behold, I have come before you! Behold, horse and the fair one! Behold, the field! Show manliness, if you are a man,' – you would say, 'God be my refuge! I am no man. What they have told you is all lies. If you are the mate, unmanliness is most comely!' A scorpion comes and raises its sting against your member, saying, 'I have heard that you are a man who laughs and is gay. Laugh, so that I may hear you laugh.' In such a case one would say, 'Now that you have come, I have no laugh and no gay temperament. What they have told you is lies. All my inclinations to laugh are preoccupied with the hope that you may go away and be far from me!'

Someone said: You sighed, and the ecstasy departed. Do not sigh, so that the ecstasy may not depart.

The Master answered: Sometimes it happens that ecstasy departs if you do not sigh, according to the various circumstances. If that had not been so, God would not have said

Abraham was a man who sighed, a clement man.

Nor would it have been right to display any act of obedience to God; for all display is ecstasy.

What you say, you say in order that ecstasy may ensue. So, if someone induces ecstasy, you attend that person in order that ecstasy may ensue. That is like shouting to a sleeper, 'Arise! It is day. The caravan is off.' Others say, 'Don't shout. He is in ecstasy. His ecstasy will start away.' The man says, 'That ecstasy is destruction, this ecstasy is deliverance from destruction.' They say, 'Don't make a confusion, for this shouting hinders thought.' The man says, 'This shouting will make the sleeper think. Otherwise what thinking will he do, whilst he is here asleep? When he has awakened, then he will start to think.'

So shouting is of two kinds. If the shouter is above the other in knowledge, his shouting will cause an increase of thought. For since his awakener is a man of knowledge and of wakefulness, when he awakens the other out of the slumber of heedlessness he informs him of his own world and draws him thither. So his thought ascends, since he has been called out of a high estate. When on the contrary the awakener is below the other in intellect, when he awakens him his gaze drops. Since his awakener is lower down, inevitably his gaze drops downwards and his thought goes to the lower world.

AJA

ACKNOWLEDGMENTS

A. J. ARBERRY (AJA)
I am the slave who set the master free
The bird on the city wall
The Sufi in the orchard
The monk who searched for a man
The thief in the orchard
The foal that would not drink
The camel, the ox and the ram
The man who stole a snake on the answer to prayer
Galen and the madman
Omar and the man who thought he saw the new moon
The grammarian and the boatman
The elephant in the dark, on the reconciliation of
     contrarieties
The parable of the anxious cow
The greedy wife and the cat
This is love
You are my life
Did I not say to you
You have seized me by the ear
Die now
Do you break our harp, exalted one
If a tree could move on foot or wing
The heart is like a grain of corn
From *Mystical Poems of Rumi*, translated by A. J. Arberry,
University of Chicago Press, 1979. Reprinted by permission of University of Chicago Press.
Two discourses are reprinted from *Discourses of Rumi*, translated by A. J. Arberry, John Murray, 1961.

COLEMAN BARKS (CB)

The guest house
My worst habit
The phrasing must change
Saladin's begging bowl
A community of the spirit
Quatrains (pp. 38–40, 81–84, 188–191)
Of being woven
The diver's clothes lying empty
The waterwheel
A mouse and a frog
The world which is made of our love for emptiness
Quietness
Story water
Solomon's crooked crown
Gnats inside the wind
The far mosque
An empty garlic
Red shirt
The three brothers and the Chinese princess
An awkward comparison
Someone digging in the ground
Tending two shops
The dog in the doorway
Acts of helplessness
The mouse and the camel
Talking through the door
A great wagon
Chickpea to cook
Enough words

Where everything is music
Dissolver of sugar

From *The Essential Rumi*, translated by Coleman Barks with John Moyne, HarperCollins USA, 1995. Reprinted with the kind permission of Coleman Barks.

ANDREW HARVEY (AH)
Quatrains (pp. 60–62, 119–121, 161–163, 231–233)
epigraph ('Anywhere you find a lullaby')

From *Love's Fire* by Andrew Harvey, Jonathan Cape, 1988. Reprinted by kind permission of Andrew Harvey.

KABIR HELMINSKI (KH)
And he is with us
You and I
Clothes abandoned on the shore
The root of the root of your Self
Search the darkness
What a man can say
The pull of love
Elegy for Sana'i
Love is reckless
Sweep the dust off the sea
Song of the reed

From *Love Is a Stranger*, translated by Kabir Helminski, ©1993. Reprinted by arrangement with Shambhala Publications, Inc., Boston, www.shambhala.com

NADER KHALILI (NK)
One by one
Look at love
How long will you hide?
All my friends
Don't be bitter my friend
In every breath
Restless
If you don't have
If you stay awake
My secret beloved
Only you
You ask me
You are drunk
You are
Everywhere
I am
Whatever happens
If you can only reflect
Where did it all go

From *Rumi: Fountain of Fire* by Nader Khalili, Cal-Earth
Books, 1994. Cal-Earth Books, 10376 Shangri La Avenue,
Hesperia, CA 92345, USA calearth@aol.com
Nader Khalili's architecture is greatly inspired by Rumi.
See http://www.calearth.org/

DANIEL LIEBERT (DL)
Come, beggars
The fragrant air
The weeping flute
As your sword
The flute weeps
We came whirling

From *Rumi: Fragments, Ecstasies*, translated by Daniel Liebert, Omega Publications, 1981. Reprinted by permission of Omega Publications.

R. A. NICHOLSON (RAN)
The marriage of true minds
The friend who said 'I'
Does personality survive?
The perfect man
The true Sufi
The birds of Solomon
Love and fear
The soul of prayer
'Here am I'
The evil in ourselves
The blind follower
The truth within us
The treasure-seeker
Fine feathers
Asleep to the world
Reality and appearance
God in nature

Amor agitate molem
Immediate knowledge
Mystics know
The relativity of evil
The soul of goodness in things evil
Good words
The complete artist
Spiritual churning
The necessary foil
Tradition and intuition
The ladder to heaven
Feeling and thinking
The carnal soul
Mystical perception
The world of time
The wine of love
The divine factory
The uses of tribulation
Remembered music
The unseen power
The ascending soul
The progress of man
The negative way
Deification

From *A Rumi Anthology*, translated by Reynold A. Nicholson, Oneworld Spiritual Classics, 2000 (ISBN 1-85168-251-1). Originally published in *Rumi, Poet and Mystic*, George Allen & Unwin, 1950. Reproduced with the kind permission of Oneworld Publications, Oxford. www.oneworld-publications.com